THE ANCIENT EGYPTIAN
— WORLD —

TEACHING GUIDE

OXFORD
UNIVERSITY PRESS

OXFORD

UNIVERSITY PRESS

Oxford University Press, Inc., publishes works that
further Oxford University's objective of excellence
in research, scholarship, and education.

Oxford   New York
Auckland   Cape Town   Dar es Salaam   Hong Kong   Karachi
Kuala Lumpur   Madrid   Melbourne   Mexico City   Nairobi
New Delhi   Shanghai   Taipei   Toronto

With offices in
Argentina   Austria   Brazil   Chile   Czech Republic   France   Greece
Guatemala   Hungary   Italy   Japan   Poland   Portugal   Singapore
South Korea   Switzerland   Thailand   Turkey   Ukraine   Vietnam

Published by Oxford University Press, Inc.
198 Madison Avenue, New York, NY, 10016
www.oup.com

Writer: Susan Moger
Editor: Robert Weisser
Project Editor: Lelia Mander
Project Director: Jacqueline A. Ball
Education Consultant: Diane L. Brooks, Ed.D.
Design: designlabnyc

Casper Grathwohl, Publisher

ISBN-13: 978-0-19-522286-9 (California edition)   ISBN-13: 978-0-19-517896-8

Printed in the United States
on acid-free paper

CONTENTS

HISTORY FROM OXFORD UNIVERSITY PRESS

"A thoroughly researched political and cultural history... makes for a solid resource for any collection."
– *School Library Journal*

THE WORLD IN ANCIENT TIMES
RONALD MELLOR AND AMANDA H. PODANY, EDS.
THE EARLY HUMAN WORLD
THE ANCIENT NEAR EASTERN WORLD
THE ANCIENT EGYPTIAN WORLD
THE ANCIENT SOUTH ASIAN WORLD
THE ANCIENT CHINESE WORLD
THE ANCIENT GREEK WORLD
THE ANCIENT ROMAN WORLD
THE ANCIENT AMERICAN WORLD

"Bringing history out of the Dark Ages!"

THE MEDIEVAL AND EARLY MODERN WORLD
BONNIE G. SMITH, ED.
THE EUROPEAN WORLD, 400-1450
THE AFRICAN AND MIDDLE EASTERN WORLD, 600-1500
THE ASIAN WORLD, 600-1500
AN AGE OF EMPIRES, 1200-1750
AN AGE OF VOYAGES, 1350-1600
AN AGE OF SCIENCE AND REVOLUTIONS, 1600-1800

"The liveliest, most realistic, most well-received American history series ever written for children."
– *Los Angeles Times*

A HISTORY OF US
JOY HAKIM
THE FIRST AMERICANS
MAKING THIRTEEEN COLONIES
FROM COLONIES TO COUNTRY
THE NEW NATION
LIBERTY FOR ALL?
WAR, TERRIBLE WAR
RECONSTRUCTING AMERICA
AN AGE OF EXTREMES
WAR, PEACE, AND ALL THAT JAZZ
ALL THE PEOPLE

FOR MORE INFORMATION, VISIT US AT WWW.OUP.COM

New from Oxford University Press
Reading History, by Janet Allen
ISBN 0-19-516595-0 hc 0-19-516596-9 pb

"*Reading History* is a great idea. I highly recommend this book."
–Dennis Denenberg, *Professor of Elementary and Early Childhood Education, Millersville University*

Strategic Methods for Content Learning
READING
HISTORY
A PRACTICAL GUIDE TO
IMPROVING LITERACY

JANET ALLEN
with Christine Landaker

NOTE TO THE TEACHER

Dear Educator:

You probably love history. You read historical novels, watch documentaries, and enjoy (and, as a history teacher, no doubt criticize) Hollywood's attempts to recreate the past. So why don't most kids love history too? We think it might be because of the tone of the history books they are assigned. Many textbook authors seem to assume that the sole goal of teaching history is to make sure the students memorize innumerable facts. So, innumerable facts are crammed onto the pages, facts without context, as thrilling to read as names in a phone book.

Real history, however, is not just facts; it's the story of real people who cared deeply about the events and controversies of their times. And learning real history is essential. It helps children to understand the events that brought the world to where they find it now. It helps them distrust stereotypes of other cultures. It helps them read critically. (It also helps them succeed in standardized assessments of their reading skills.) We, like you, find history positively addictive. Students can feel the same way. (Can you imagine a child reading a history book with a flashlight after lights out, just because it is so interesting?)

The World in Ancient Times books reveal ancient history to be a great story—a whole bunch of great stories—some of which have been known for centuries, but some of which are just being discovered. Each book in the series is written by a team of two writers: a scholar who is working in the field of ancient history and knows what is new and exciting, and a well-known children's book author who knows how to communicate these ideas to kids. The teams have come up with books that are historically accurate and up to date as well as beautifully written. They also feature magnificent illustrations of real artifacts, archaeological sites, and works of art, along with maps and timelines to allow readers to get a sense of where events are set in place and time. Etymologies from the *Oxford English Dictionary*, noted in the margins, help to expand students' vocabulary by identifying the ancient roots, along with the meanings, of English words.

The authors of our books use vivid language to describe what we know and to present the evidence for *how* we know what we know. We let the readers puzzle right along with the historians and archaeologists. The evidence comes in the form of primary sources, not only in the illustrations but especially in the documents written in ancient times, which are quoted extensively.

You can integrate these primary sources into lessons with your students. When they read a document or look at an artifact or building in the illustrations they can pose questions and make hypotheses about the culture it came from. Why was a king shown as much larger than his attendants in an Egyptian relief sculpture? Why was Pliny unsure about what to do with accused Christians in his letter to the emperor? In this way, students can think like historians.

The series provides a complete narrative for a yearlong course on ancient history. You might choose to have your students read all eight narrative books as they learn about each of the civilizations in turn (or fewer than eight, depending on the ancient civilizations covered in your school's curriculum). Or you might choose to highlight certain chapters in each of the books, and use the others for extended activities or research projects. Since each chapter is written to stand on its own, the students will not be confused if you don't assign all of them. The *Primary Sources and Reference Volume* provides longer primary sources than are available in the other books, allowing students to make their own interpretations and comparisons across cultures.

The ancient world was the stage on which many institutions that we think of as modern were first played out: law, cities, legitimate government, technology, and so on. The major world religions all had their origins long ago, before 600 CE, as did many of the great cities of the world. *The World in Ancient Times* presents this ancient past in a new way—new not just to young adults, but to any audience. The scholarship is top-notch and the telling will catch you up in the thrill of exploration and discovery.

Amanda H. Podany and Ronald Mellor
General Editors, *The World in Ancient Times*

THE WORLD IN ANCIENT TIMES PROGRAM

I. STUDENT EDITION

- ► Engaging, friendly narrative
- ► A wide range of primary sources in every chapter
- ► The authority of Oxford scholarship
- ► Period illustrations and specially commissioned maps

II. TEACHING GUIDE

- ► Wide range of activities and classroom approaches
- ► Strategies for universal access and improving literacy (ELL, struggling readers, advanced learners)
- ► Multiple assessment tools

III. STUDENT STUDY GUIDE

- ► Exercises correlated to Student Edition and Teaching Guide
- ► Portfolio approach
- ► Activities for every level of learning
- ► Literacy through reading and writing

PRIMARY SOURCES AND REFERENCE VOLUME

- ► Broad selection of primary sources in each subject area
- ► Ideal resource for in-class exercises and unit projects

TEACHING GUIDE: **KEY FEATURES**

The Teaching Guides organize each *The World in Ancient Times* book into units, usually of three or four chapters each. The chapters in each unit cover a key span of time or have a common theme, such as a civilization's origins, government, religion, economy, and daily life.

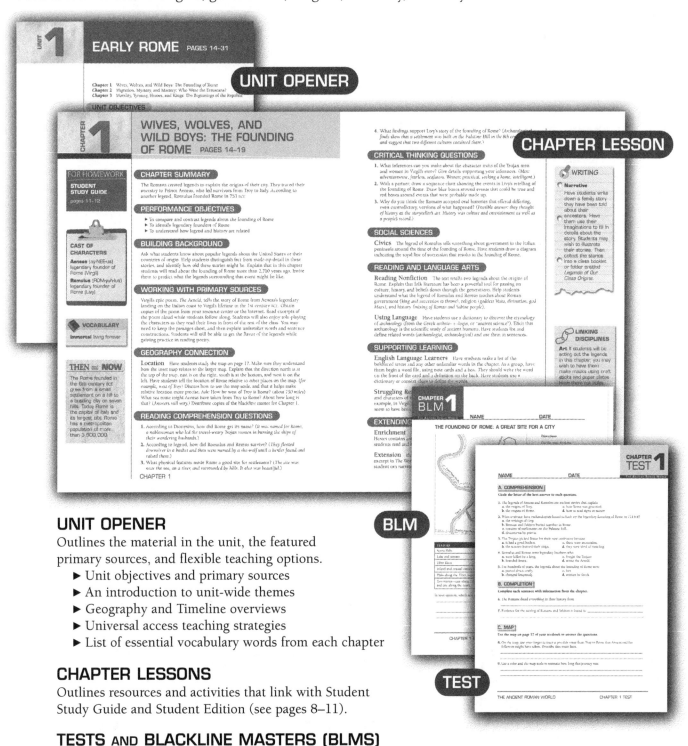

UNIT OPENER

Outlines the material in the unit, the featured primary sources, and flexible teaching options.

► Unit objectives and primary sources
► An introduction to unit-wide themes
► Geography and Timeline overviews
► Universal access teaching strategies
► List of essential vocabulary words from each chapter

CHAPTER LESSONS

Outlines resources and activities that link with Student Study Guide and Student Edition (see pages 8–11).

TESTS AND BLACKLINE MASTERS (BLMS)

Reproducible tests and exercises for assessment, homework, or classroom projects

Organized so that you can easily find the information you need.

CHAPTER SUMMARY AND PERFORMANCE OBJECTIVES

The Chapter Summary gives an overview of the information in the chapter. The Performance Objectives are the three or four important goals students should achieve in the chapter. Accomplishing these goals will help students master the information in the book.

BUILDING BACKGROUND

This section connects students to the chapter they are about to read. Students may be asked to use what they know to make predictions about the text, preview the images in the chapter, or connect modern life with the ancient subject matter.

WORKING WITH PRIMARY SOURCES

A major feature of *The World in Ancient Times* is having students read about history through the words and images of the people who lived it. Each book includes excerpts from the best sources from these ancient civilizations, giving the narrative an immediacy that is difficult to match in secondary sources. Students can read further in these sources on their own or in small groups using the accompanying *The World in Ancient Times Primary Sources and Reference Volume*. The Teaching Guide recommends activities so students of all skill levels can appreciate the ways people from the past saw themselves, their ideas and values, and their fears and dreams.

CHAPTER 1

WIVES, WOLVES, AND WILD BOYS: THE FOUNDING OF ROME PAGES 14–19

FOR HOMEWORK

STUDENT STUDY GUIDE
pages 11–12

CAST OF CHARACTERS

Aeneas (ay-NEE-us) legendary founder of Rome (Virgil)

Romulus (ROM-yuh-lus) legendary founder of Rome (Livy)

VOCABULARY

immortal living forever

THEN and **NOW**

The Rome founded in the 8th century BCE grew from a small settlement on a hill to a bustling city on seven hills. Today Rome is the capital of Italy and its largest city. Rome has a metropolitan population of more than 3,500,000.

CHAPTER SUMMARY

The Romans created legends to explain the origins of their city. They traced their ancestry to Prince Aeneas, who led survivors from Troy to Italy. According to another legend, Romulus founded Rome in 753 BCE.

PERFORMANCE OBJECTIVES

- ▶ To compare and contrast legends about the founding of Rome
- ▶ To identify legendary founders of Rome
- ▶ To understand how legend and history are related

BUILDING BACKGROUND

Ask what students know about popular legends about the United States or their countries of origin. Help students distinguish fact from made-up detail in these stories, and identify how old these stories might be. Explain that in this chapter students will read about the founding of Rome more than 2,700 years ago. Invite them to predict what the legends surrounding that event might be like.

WORKING WITH PRIMARY SOURCES

Virgil's epic poem, *The Aeneid*, tells the story of Rome from Aeneas's legendary landing on the Italian coast to Virgil's lifetime in the 1st century BCE. Obtain copies of the poem from your resource center or the Internet. Read excerpts of the poem aloud while students follow along. Students will also enjoy role-playing the characters as they read their lines in front of the rest of the class. You may need to keep the passages short, and then explain unfamiliar words and sentence constructions. Students will still be able to get the flavor of the legends while gaining practice in reading poetry.

GEOGRAPHY CONNECTION

Location Have students study the map on page 17. Make sure they understand how the inset map relates to the larger map. Explain that the direction north is at the top of the map, east is on the right, south is at the bottom, and west is on the left. Have students tell the location of Rome relative to other places on the map. (*for example, west of Troy*) Discuss how to use the map scale, and that it helps make relative location more precise. Ask: How far west of Troy is Rome? (*about 750 miles*) What sea route might Aeneas have taken from Troy to Rome? About how long is that? (*Answers will vary.*) Distribute copies of the blackline master for Chapter 1.

READING COMPREHENSION QUESTIONS

1. According to Dionysius, how did Rome get its name? (*It was named for Roma, a noblewoman who led the travel-weary Trojan women in burning the ships of their wandering husbands.*)
2. According to legend, how did Romulus and Remus survive? (*They floated downriver in a basket and then were nursed by a she-wolf until a herder found and raised them.*)
3. What physical features made Rome a good site for settlement? (*The site was near the sea, on a river, and surrounded by hills. It also was beautiful.*)

CHAPTER 1

GEOGRAPHY CONNECTION

Each chapter has a Geography Connection to strengthen students' map skills as well as their understanding of how geography affects human civilization. One of the five themes of geography (Location, Interaction, Movement, Place, and Regions) is highlighted in each chapter. Map skills such as reading physical, political, and historical maps; using latitude and longitude to find locations; and using the features of a map (mileage scale, legend) are taught throughout the book and reinforced in blackline masters.

4. What findings support Livy's story of the founding of Rome? (*Archaeological finds show that a settlement was built on the Palatine Hill in the 8th century BCE and suggest that two different cultures coexisted there.*)

CRITICAL THINKING QUESTIONS

1. What inferences can you make about the character traits of the Trojan men and women in Virgil's story? Give details supporting your inferences. (*Men: adventuresome, fearless, seafarers. Women: practical, seeking a home, intelligent.*)
2. With a partner, draw a sequence chart showing the events in Livy's retelling of the founding of Rome. Draw blue boxes around events that could be true and red boxes around events that were probably made up.
3. Why do you think the Romans accepted oral histories that offered differing, even contradictory, versions of what happened? (*Possible answer: they thought of history as the storyteller's art. History was culture and entertainment as well as a people's record.*)

SOCIAL SCIENCES

Civics   The legend of Romulus tells something about government in the Italian peninsula around the time of the founding of Rome. Have students draw a diagram indicating the royal line of succession that results in the founding of Rome.

READING AND LANGUAGE ARTS

Reading Nonfiction   The text retells two legends about the origins of Rome. Explain that folk literature has been a powerful tool for passing on culture, history, and beliefs down through the generations. Help students understand what the legend of Romulus and Remus teaches about Roman government (*king and succession to throne*), religion (*goddess Vesta, divination, and Mars*), and history (*mixing of Roman and Sabine people*).

Using Language   Have students use a dictionary to discover the etymology of *archaeology* (from the Greek *archaio-* + *-logia*, or "ancient science"). Elicit that archaeology is the scientific study of ancient humans. Have students list and define related words (*archaeologist, archaeological*) and use them in sentences.

SUPPORTING LEARNING

English Language Learners   Have students make a list of the boldfaced terms and any other unfamiliar words in the chapter. As a group, have them begin a word file, using note cards and a box. They should write the word on the front of the card and a definition on the back. Have students use a dictionary or context clues to define the words.

Struggling Readers   Have students make a chart comparing the events and characters of the two legends. Then help students draw conclusions: for example, in Virgil, the founders of Rome came from Troy; in Livy, the founders seem to have been living in Italy already.

EXTENDING LEARNING

Enrichment   Edith Hamilton's book *Mythology: Timeless Tales of Gods and Heroes* contains another myth about the founding of Rome by Aeneas. Have students read and summarize this myth for the class.

Extension   Have student groups act out scenes from *The Aeneid*, from the excerpt in *The World in Ancient Times Primary Sources and Reference Volume*. One student can narrate while the others take the parts of the characters involved.

THE ANCIENT ROMAN WORLD

WRITING

Narrative

Have students write down a family story they have been told about their ancestors. Have them use their imaginations to fill in details about the story. Students may wish to illustrate their stories. Then collect the stories into a class booklet or folder entitled *Legends of Our Class Origins.*

LINKING DISCIPLINES

Art If students will be acting out the legends in this chapter, you may wish to have them make masks using craft sticks and paper plates. Have them cut holes for eyes and mouth. They can model their characters' features after the pictures of Roman men and women in Chapters 1–3.

READING COMPREHENSION AND CRITICAL THINKING QUESTIONS

The reading comprehension questions are general enough to allow free-flowing class or small group discussion, yet specific enough to be used for oral or written assessment of students' grasp of the important information. The critical thinking questions are intended to engage students in a deeper analysis of the text and can also be used for oral or written assessment.

SOCIAL SCIENCES ACTIVITIES

Students can use these activities to connect the subject matter in the Student Edition with other areas in the social sciences: economics, civics, and science, technology, and society.

READING AND LANGUAGE ARTS

These activities serve a twofold purpose: Some are designed to facilitate the development of nonfiction reading strategies. Others can be used to help students' appreciation of fiction and poetry, as well as nonfiction, by dealing with concepts such as word choice, description, and figurative language.

SUPPORTING LEARNING AND EXTENDING LEARNING

Each chapter gives suggestions for students of varying abilities and learning styles; for example, advanced learners, below-level readers, auditory/visual/tactile learners, and English language learners. These may be individual, partner, or group activities, and may or may not require your ongoing supervision.
(For more on Supporting or Extending Learning sections, see pages 16–19.)

Icons quickly help to identify key concepts, facts, activities, and assessment activities in the sidebars.

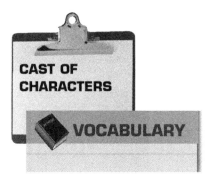

▶ Cast of Characters/Vocabulary

These sidebars point out and identify bolded, curriculum-specific vocabulary words and significant personalities in the chapter. Pronunciation guides are included where necessary. Additional important vocabulary words are listed in each unit opener.

▶ Writing

Each chapter has a suggestion for a specific writing assignment. You can make these assignments as you see fit—to help students meet state requirements in writing as well as to help individual students improve their skills. Areas of writing covered include the following:

Description	Personal writing (journal/diary)
Narration	News article (print and electronic)
Explanation	Dialogue
Persuasion	Interview
Composition	Poetry

▶ Then and Now

This feature provides interesting facts and ideas about the ancient civilization and relates it to the modern world. This may be an aspect of government that we still use today, word origins of common modern expressions, physical reminders of the past that are still evident, and other features. You can use this item simply to promote interest in the subject matter or as a springboard to other research.

▶ Linking Disciplines

This feature offers opportunities to investigate other subject areas that relate to the material in the Student Edition: math, science, arts, and health. Specific areas of these subjects are emphasized: **Math** (arithmetic, algebra, geometry, data, statistics); **Science** (life science, earth science, physical science); **Arts** (music, arts, dance, drama, architecture); **Health** (personal health, world health).

▶ For Homework

A quick glance links you to additional activities in the Student Study Guide that can be assigned as homework.

ASSESSMENT

The World in Ancient Times program intentionally omits from the Student Edition the kinds of section, chapter, and unit questions that are used to review and assess learning in standard textbooks. It is the purpose of the series to engage readers in learning—and loving—history written as good literature. Rather than interrupting student reading, and enjoyment, all assessment instruments for the series have been placed in the Teaching Guides.

▶ CHAPTER TESTS

A reproducible chapter test follows each chapter in this Teaching Guide. These tests will help you assess students' mastery of the content standards addressed in each chapter. These tests measure a variety of cognitive and analytical skills, particularly comprehension, critical thinking, and expository writing, through multiple choice, short answer, and essay questions.

An answer key for the chapter tests is provided at the end of the Teaching Guide.

▶ WRAP-UP TEST

After the last chapter test you will find a wrap-up test consisting of 10 essay questions that evaluate students' ability to synthesize and express what they've learned about the ancient civilization under study.

▶ RUBRICS

The rubrics at the back of this Teaching Guide will help you assess students' written work, oral presentations, and group projects. They include a Scoring Rubric, based on the California State Public School standards for good writing and effective cooperative learning. In addition, a simplified hand-out is provided, plus a form for evaluating group projects and a Library/Media Center Research Log to help students focus and evaluate their research. Students can also evaluate their own work using these rubrics.

▶ BLACKLINE MASTERS (BLMs)

A blackline master follows each chapter in the Teaching Guide. These BLMs are reproducible pages for you to use as in-class activities or homework exercises. They can also be used for assessment as needed.

▶ ADDITIONAL ASSESSMENT ACTIVITIES

Each unit opener includes suggestions for using one or more unit projects for assessment. These points, and the rubrics provided, will help you evaluate how your students are progressing towards meeting the unit objectives.

USING THE STUDENT STUDY GUIDE FOR ASSESSMENT

▶ Study Guide Activities

Assignments in the Student Study Guide correspond with those in the Teaching Guide. If needed, these Student Study Guide activities can be used for assessment.

▶ Portfolio Approach

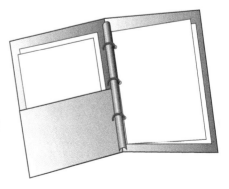

Student Study Guide pages can be removed from the workbook and turned in for grading. When the pages are returned, they can be part of the students' individual history journals. Have students keep a 3-ring binder portfolio of Study Guide pages, alongside writing projects and other activities.

STUDENT STUDY GUIDE: **KEY FEATURES**

The Student Study Guide works as both standalone instructional material and as a support to the Student Edition and this Teaching Guide. Certain activities encourage informal small-group or family participation. These features make it an effective teaching tool:

Flexibility

You can use the Study Guide in the classroom, with individuals or small groups, or send it home for homework. You can distribute the entire guide to students; however, the pages are perforated so you can remove and distribute only the pertinent lessons.

A page on reports and special projects in the front of the Study Guide directs students to the Further Reading resource in the student edition. This feature gives students general guidance on doing research and devising independent study projects of their own.

FACSIMILE SPREAD
The Study Guide begins with a facsimile spread from the Student Edition. This spread gives reading strategies and highlights key features: captions, primary sources, sidebars, headings, etymologies. The spread supplies the contextualization students need to fully understand the material.

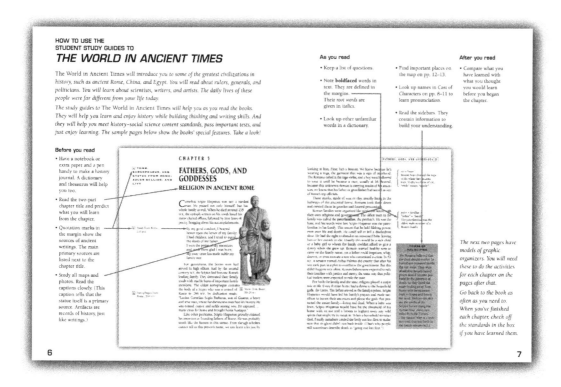

Portfolio Approach

The Study Guide pages are three-hole-punched so they can be integrated with notebook paper in a looseleaf binder. This history journal or portfolio can become both a record of content mastery and an outlet for each student's unique creative expression. Responding to prompts, students can write poetry or songs, plays and character sketches, create storyboards or cartoons, or construct multi-layered timelines.

The portfolio approach gives students unlimited opportunities for practice in areas that need strengthening. Students cam share their journals and compare their work. And the Study Guide pages in the portfolio make a valuable assessment tool for you. It is an ongoing record of performance that can be reviewed and graded periodically.

GRAPHIC ORGANIZERS

This feature contains reduced models of seven graphic organizers referenced frequently in the guide. Using these devices will help students organize the material so it is meaningful to them. (Full-size reproducibles of each graphic organizer are provided at the back of this Teaching Guide.) These graphic organizers include: outline, main idea map, K-W-L chart (What I Know, What I Want to Know, What I Learned), Venn diagram, timeline, sequence of events chart, and T-chart.

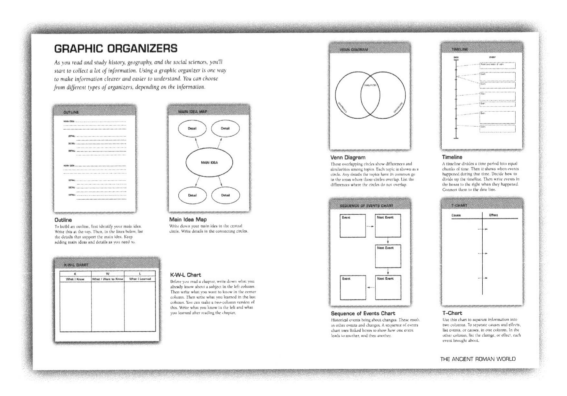

Each chapter lesson is designed to draw students into the subject matter. Recurring features and exercises challenge their knowledge and allow them to practice valuable analysis skills. Activities in the Teaching Guide and Student Study Guide complement but do not duplicate each other. Together they offer a wide range of class work, group projects, and opportunities for further study and assessment that can be tailored to all ability levels.

CHAPTER SUMMARY
briefly reviews big ideas from the chapter.

ACCESS
invites students into the content by building background, tapping prior knowledge, or visual note-taking.

ADDITIONAL VOCABULARY
Additional vocabulary words important to accessing student book content are listed on page 10 of every Student Study Guide.

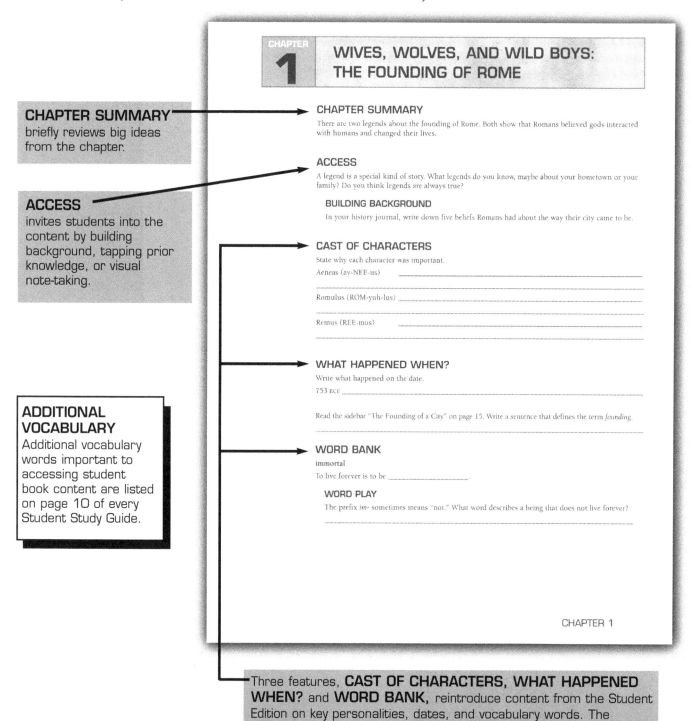

CHAPTER 1 — WIVES, WOLVES, AND WILD BOYS: THE FOUNDING OF ROME

CHAPTER SUMMARY
There are two legends about the founding of Rome. Both show that Romans believed gods interacted with humans and changed their lives.

ACCESS
A legend is a special kind of story. What legends do you know, maybe about your hometown or your family? Do you think legends are always true?

BUILDING BACKGROUND
In your history journal, write down five beliefs Romans had about the way their city came to be.

CAST OF CHARACTERS
State why each character was important.
Aeneas (ay-NEE-us) _____
Romulus (ROM-yuh-lus) _____
Remus (REE-mus) _____

WHAT HAPPENED WHEN?
Write what happened on the date.
753 BCE _____

Read the sidebar "The Founding of a City" on page 15. Write a sentence that defines the term *founding*.

WORD BANK
immortal
To live forever is to be _____.

WORD PLAY
The prefix *im-* sometimes means "not." What word describes a being that does not live forever?
_____

CHAPTER 1

Three features, **CAST OF CHARACTERS, WHAT HAPPENED WHEN?** and **WORD BANK**, reintroduce content from the Student Edition on key personalities, dates, and vocabulary words. The Teaching Guide also reinforces this information chapter-by-chapter in the VOCABULARY and CAST OF CHARACTERS sidebars.

CRITICAL THINKING
CAUSE AND EFFECT
Draw a line from each cause and connect it to the result, or effect. (There is one extra effect.)

CAUSE	EFFECT
1. Amulius feared he would be overthrown,	a. they floated down the river and were saved by a she-wolf.
2. Rhea Silvia broke her vows,	b. the Romans and Sabines went to war.
3. A servant couldn't kill the babies,	c. Romulus killed Remus.
4. Remus made fun of Romulus,	d. Romans and Sabines called a truce.
5. Romulus's men kidnapped Sabine women,	e. Romulus and Remus were born.
6. The Sabine women ran onto the battlefield,	f. he forced Rhea Silvia to join the Vestal Virgins.
	g. Remus killed Romulus.

WITH A PARENT OR PARTNER
When you have completed the chart, read aloud each cause-and-effect pairing to a parent or partner. Use the word "so" to connect each cause with each effect.

WRITE ABOUT IT
The Trojan women were *appalled* that Aeneas and the Trojan men were planning another journey after they reached the mouth of the Tiber River. To be *appalled* means to be

a) happy.

b) excited.

c) shocked.

Circle your answer.

In your history journal, write a short dialogue or a descriptive scene between the Trojan men and women about making this second journey. Why were the women appalled? How did the men respond?

WORKING WITH PRIMARY SOURCES
The image at left is an ancient Roman coin. It shows an image of a Roman god. Think about what we can learn about ancient cultures through artifacts like this one. Answer the following questions in your history journal.

1. Why do you think the figure is wearing an olive wreath?

2. Why would the Romans put a god on their coins?

3. What famous people do we use on coins today? (It's okay to take a peek at your pocket change!)

4. If people found your coins hundreds of years from now, what conclusions might they draw about your culture?

5. Think up a design for your own coin and draw it in your history journal.

THE ANCIENT ROMAN WORLD

CRITICAL THINKING exercises draw on such thinking skills as establishing cause and effect, making inferences, drawing conclusions, determining sequence of events, comparing and contrasting, identifying main ideas and details, and other analytical process.

WRITE ABOUT IT gives students writing suggestions drawn from the material. A writing assignment may stem from a vocabulary word, a historical event, or a reading of a primary source. The assignment can take any number of forms: newspaper article, letter, short essay, a scene with dialogue, a diary entry.

WORKING WITH PRIMARY SOURCES invites students to read primary sources closely. Exercises include answering comprehension questions, evaluating point of view, and writing and other forms of creative expression, including music, art, and design. "In Your Own Words" writing activities ask students to paraphrase a primary source.

The books in this series are written in a lively, narrative style to inspire a love of reading history–social science. English language learners and struggling readers are given special consideration within the program's exercises and activities. And students who love to read and learn will also benefit from the program's rich and varied material. Following are strategies to make sure each and every student gets the most out of the subjects you will teach through *The World in Ancient Times*.

ENGLISH LANGUAGE LEARNERS

For English learners to achieve academic success, the instructional considerations for teachers include two mandates:

- Help them attain grade level, content area knowledge, and academic language.
- Provide for the development of English language proficiency.

To accomplish these goals, you should plan lessons that reflect the student's level of English proficiency. Students progress through five developmental levels as they increase in language proficiency:

Beginning and Early Intermediate (*grade level material will be mostly incomprehensible, students need a great deal of teacher support*)

Intermediate (*grade level work will be a challenge*)

Early Advanced and Advanced (*close to grade level reading and writing, students continue to need support*)

The books in this program are written at the intermediate level. However, you can still use the lesson plans for students of different levels by using the strategies below:

Tap Prior Knowledge
What students know about the topic will help determine your next steps for instruction. Using K-W-L charts, brainstorming, and making lists are ways to find out what they know. English learners bring a rich cultural diversity into the classroom. By sharing what they know, students can connect their knowledge and experiences to the course.

Set the Context
Use different tools to make new information understandable. These can be images, artifacts, maps, timelines, illustrations, charts, videos, or graphic organizers. Techniques such as role-playing and story-boarding can also be helpful. Speak in shorter sentences, with careful enunciation, expanded explanations, repetitions, and paraphrasing. Use fewer idiomatic expressions.

Show—Don't Just Tell
English learners often get lost as they listen to directions, explanations, lectures, and discussions. By showing students what is expected, you can help them participate more fully in classroom activities. Students need to be shown how to use the graphic organizers in this guide and the mini versions in the student study guide, as well as other blackline masters for note-taking and practice. An overhead transparency with whole or small groups is also effective.

Use the Text

Because of unfamiliar words, students will need help. Teach them to preview the chapter using text features (headings, bold print, sidebars, italics). See the suggestions in the facsimile of the Student Edition, shown on pages 6–7 of the Student Study Guide. Show students organizing structures such as cause and effect or comparing and contrasting. Have students read to each other in pairs. Encourage them to share their history journals with each other. Use Read Aloud/Think Aloud, perhaps with an overhead transparency. Help them create word banks, charts, and graphic organizers. Discuss the main idea after reading.

Check for Understanding

Rather than simply ask students if they understand, stop frequently and ask them to paraphrase or expand on what you just said. Such techniques will give you a much clearer assessment of their understanding.

Provide for Interaction

As students interact with the information and speak their thoughts, their content knowledge and academic language skills improve. Increase interaction in the classroom through cooperative learning, small group work, and partner share. By working and talking with others, students can practice asking and answering questions.

Use Appropriate Assessment

When modifying the instruction, you will also need to modify the assessment. Multiple choice, true and false, and other criterion reference tests are suitable, but consider changing test format and structure. English learners are constantly improving their language proficiency in their oral and written responses, but they are often grammatically incorrect. Remember to be thoughtful and fair about giving students credit for their content knowledge and use of academic language, even if their English isn't perfect.

STRUGGLING READERS

Some students struggle to understand the information presented in a textbook. The following strategies for content-area reading can help students improve their ability to make comparisons, sequence events, determine importance, summarize, evaluate, synthesize, analyze, and solve problems.

Build Knowledge of Genre

Both the fiction and narrative nonfiction genres are incorporated into *The World in Ancient Times*. This combination of genres makes the text interesting and engaging. But teachers must be sure students can identify and use the organizational structures of both genres.

Fiction	Nonfiction
Each chapter is a story	Content: historical information
Setting: historical time and place	Organizational structure: cause/effect, sequence of events, problem/solution
Characters: historical figures	Other features: maps, timelines, sidebars, photographs, primary sources
Plot: problems, roadblocks, and resolutions	

In addition, the textbook has a wealth of the text features of nonfiction: bold and italic print, sidebars, headings and subheadings, labels, captions, and "signal words" such as *first*, *next*, and *finally*. Teaching these organizational structures and text features is essential for struggling readers.

Build Background

Having background information about a topic makes reading about it so much easier. When students lack background information, teachers can preteach or "front load" concepts and vocabulary, using a variety of instructional techniques. Conduct a chapter or book walk, looking at titles, headings, and other text features to develop a big picture of the content. Focus on new vocabulary words during the "walk" and create a word bank with illustrations for future reference. Read aloud key passages and discuss the meaning. Focus on the timeline and maps to help students develop a sense of time and place. Show a video, go to a website, and have trade books and magazines on the topic available for student exploration.

Comprehension Strategies

While reading, successful readers are predicting, making connections, monitoring, visualizing, questioning, inferring, and summarizing. Struggling readers have a harder time with these "in the head" processes. The following strategies will help these students construct meaning from the text until they are able to do it on their own.

PREDICT: Before reading, conduct a picture and text feature "tour" of the chapter to make predictions. Ask students if they remember if this has ever happened before, to predict what might happen this time.

MAKE CONNECTIONS: Help students relate content to their background (text to text, text to self, and text to the world).

MONITOR AND CONFIRM: Encourage students to stop reading when they come across an unknown word, phrase, or concept. In their notebooks, have them make a note of text they don't understand and ask for clarification or figure it out. While this activity slows down reading at first, it is effective in improving skills over time.

VISUALIZE: Students benefit from imagining the events described in a story. Sketching scenes, story-boarding, role-playing, and looking for sensory details all help students with this strategy.

INFER: Help students look beyond the literal meaning of a text to understand deeper meanings. Graphic organizers and discussions provide opportunities to broaden their understanding. Looking closely at the "why" of historical events helps students infer.

QUESTION AND DISCUSS: Have students jot down their questions as they read, and then share them during discussions. Or have students come up with the type of questions they think a teacher would ask. Over time students will develop more complex inferential questions, which lead to group discussions. Questioning and discussing also helps students see ideas from multiple perspectives and draw conclusions, both critical skills for understanding history.

DETERMINE IMPORTANCE: Teach students how to decide what is most important from all the facts and details in nonfiction. After reading for an overall understanding, they can go back to highlight important ideas, words, and phrases. Clues for determining importance include bold or italic print, signal words, and other text features. A graphic organizer such as a main idea map also helps.

Teach and Practice Decoding Strategies

Rather than simply defining an unfamiliar word, teach struggling readers decoding strategies:

- Have them look at the prefix, suffix, and root to help figure out the new word.

- Look for words they know within the word.

- Use the context for clues, and read further or reread.

ADVANCED LEARNERS

Every classroom has students who finish the required assignments and then want additional challenges. Fortunately, the very nature of history and social science offers a wide range of opportunities for students to explore topics in greater depth. Encourage them to come up with their own ideas for an additional assignment. Determine the final product, its presentation, and a timeline for completion.

▶ Research

Students can develop in-depth understanding through seeking information, exploring ideas, asking and answering questions, making judgments, considering points of view, and evaluating actions and events. They will need access to a wide range of resource materials: the Internet, maps, encyclopedias, trade books, magazines, dictionaries, artifacts, newspapers, museum catalogues, brochures, and the library. See the Further Reading section at the end of the Student Edition for good jumping-off points.

▶ Projects

You can encourage students to capitalize on their strengths as learners (visual, verbal, kinesthetic, or musical) or to try a new way of responding. Students can prepare a debate or write a persuasive paper, play, skit, poem, song, dance, game, puzzle, or biography. They can create an alphabet book on the topic, film a video, do a book talk, or illustrate a book. They can render charts, graphs, or other visual representations. Allow for creativity and support students' thinking.

Cheryl A. Caldera, M.A.
Literacy Coach

PREDYNASTIC EGYPT TO THE OLD KINGDOM
PAGES 14–40

UNIT OBJECTIVES

Unit 1 covers the period in Egyptian history from the time of the first king, Narmer, who united Upper and Lower Egypt, through the reign of King Djoser, who built the first pyramid. In this unit, your students will learn

▶ why the Nile River was so important to Egyptians.
▶ the powers of the early kings, such as Pepi II.
▶ how Egypt's power and wealth grew.
▶ the significance of the Palette of Narmer.
▶ information about the design and construction of the first pyramid.
▶ what hieroglyphics are and the importance of the Rosetta Stone in deciphering them.

PRIMARY SOURCES

Unit 1 includes pictures of artifacts/excerpts from the following primary sources:

▶ *Hymn to the Nile*
▶ Nilometer
▶ Inscription on the tomb of Harkhuf
▶ Palette of Narmer Inscriptions at Sehel near Aswan
▶ Edwin Smith Papyrus
▶ Pyramid texts
▶ Clay tablets from Abydos
▶ Inscriptions on stones and statues
▶ *Satire of the Trades*
▶ Rosetta Stone

BIG IDEAS IN UNIT 1

Environment, trade, and **power** are the big ideas presented in Unit 1. In the Nile River Valley, periodic floods deposited rich soil that farmers depended on to grow increasing amounts of crops. The agricultural abundance of this environment resulted in the growth of trade and wealth, and the consolidation of power in the hands of rulers. The unit discusses the power wielded by the early kings of Egypt and the symbols of that power, such as the pyramid of Djoser.

GEOGRAPHY CONNECTION

Refer students to the map of ancient Egypt on pages 11–12—the Nile Valley and surrounding lands. Make sure they understand the significance of the Nile's periodic floods and can trace the Nile from its source to the Delta. Students should be able to explain that the Nile is unusual in that it flows from south to north. Comparing a map of the Nile Valley in ancient Egypt to a map of the Nile Valley today, have students identify the dam at Aswan and Lake Nasser, a project that profoundly changed the Nile River and Egypt itself.

TIMELINE

3150 BCE	King Scorpion rules; Dynasty 0
3100 BCE	Narmer/Menes unifies Egypt
3050 BCE	Aha rules; first king of Dynasty 1
About 3000 BCE	Writing begins in Egypt
2700 BCE	Old Kingdom Period begins (dynasties 3–6)
2668–2649 BCE	Rule of Djoser; first pyramid built

UNIT PROJECTS

Egyptian History "On Line"

Invite a team of students to create a timeline of the "Top 10" periods in Egyptian history. (See sidebar, page 28.) Have them copy the dates and period information onto separate index cards, using a different color for each period. Stretch a line of monofilament or string along a wall and have students attach the cards in chronological order with paper clips or string. As students learn more about each period, other groups can add information to the timeline.

Technology News

Ask small groups of students to research, write, and illustrate articles for an ancient Egyptian technology newsletter. Articles can focus on innovations introduced in Unit 1: nilometer, shaduf, irrigation channel, Step Pyramid, and papyrus. Using the blackline master for Chapter 4 (page 42), they can sign the articles with their names in hieroglyphs.

George Washington Palette

Invite groups of students to create a cardboard palette the same size (two feet tall) and shape as the Palette of Narmer shown on page 24. Students can paint their palette dark green and place George Washington's name in a box at the top on both sides. Then they can draw scenes from Washington's life—two scenes on the front and three on the back. Encourage students to think of symbols to incorporate on the palette, such as an eagle and an early American flag.

Interview with Imhotep

Imhotep has agreed to appear before a panel of students in your class. (He will bring his advisers with him.) Create two teams of students—the panelists on one team, Imhotep and his advisers on the other. Teams can use information from Chapter 3 as well as library/media center and online resources as the basis for questions and responses about the Step Pyramid and Imhotep's life. Useful websites about Imhotep and the Step Pyramid can be found in the Websites section at the back of students' books.

ADDITIONAL ASSESSMENT

For Unit 1, divide the class into groups and have them all undertake the Technology News project. In particular, note how students' news reports explain how the technology either helped Egypt grow in wealth and power or was a symbol of the country's increasing wealth and power. Use the scoring rubric at the back of this guide to assess students' work, and have students rate their own work with the self-assessment rubric.

LITERATURE CONNECTION

There are numerous copies of *The Hymn to the Nile* available online. (Some sources call it The Hymn to the Nile Flood.) Students can read the complete version in groups to understand further how the Egyptians felt about the Nile. One on-line source of the hymn is *www.touregypt.net/hymntothenile.htm*. The same site lists other literature from ancient Egypt: *www.touregypt.net/literature.htm*. In addition, students can learn more from these secondary sources:

▶ Payne, Elizabeth Ann. *Pharaohs of Ancient Egypt*. New York: Random House Books for Young Readers, 1981. This book for young readers discusses the life and history of ancient Egypt from earliest times through the reign of Ramesses II.

▶ Giblin, James Cross. *Riddle of the Rosetta Stone: Key to Ancient Egypt*. Rebound by Sagebrush, 1999. A straightforward account of how the Rosetta Stone, containing Greek, Egyptian, and hieroglyphics, allowed scholars to understand a once unknown language.

▶ Sands, Emily. *Egyptology*. Candlewick Press, 2004. This illustrated book is mainly factual in content, meant as a guide through a fascinating journal from an Egyptologist in the 1920s.

UNIVERSAL ACCESS

The following strategies are designed to cover a range of learning styles and reading, language, and skill levels. This section includes suggestions for differentiating instruction to meet the diverse needs of your students.

Reading Strategies

▶ To facilitate reading, point out features such as illustrations, information, and definitions in the side columns that students will encounter as they read. For example, Pharaoh Who? on page 14, Topsy-Turvy on page 23, and the Step Pyramid and Rosetta Stone illustrations on pages 30 and 39.

▶ Call on students to read sections of the chapters aloud. For example, the description of farmers irrigating and planting fields along the Nile (page 17) or King Djoser's tour of the Step Pyramid (page 32). Encourage students to make their voices expressive and to use hand gestures where appropriate. Fit the reading passage to the abilities of each student.

Writing Strategies

▶ Have partners make a three-column chart with headings for each of the unit's big ideas. Partners should get together after reading each chapter to jot down their observations in each category.

▶ Have students create a cause and effect chart (see the T-chart with the graphic organizers at the back of this guide) showing how the rise and fall of the Nile River affected farmers in the Nile Valley.

Listening and Speaking Strategies

▶ As you read portions of the chapters, call on volunteers to describe what they think the scenes looked like; for example, watching the Nile rise (page 16) or learning to be a scribe (pages 36–37).

▶ Encourage a group of students to prepare and present a "Person on the Street" interview involving a reporter for an Egyptian newspaper and workers at the site of King Djoser's Step Pyramid. The question could be, "What do you like (dislike) most about the job?" Responders should mention on-the-job injuries and treatments described on page 33.

UNIT VOCABULARY LIST

The following words that appear in Unit 1 are important for your students' understanding of the social studies content as well as for development of literacy. Use these words for vocabulary study or to reinforce language arts skills (e.g., synonyms, compound words, prefixes and suffixes, and related words). The words are listed below in the order in which they appear in the chapters.

Chapter 1	Chapter 2	Chapter 3	Chapter 4
wielding	shriveled	unwieldy	scribe
barren	palette	manageable	apprentice
relentless	gateway	dynasty	privileged
sacred	unification	chaos	breakthrough
highlands	symbolize	divine	fluent
obsessively	harmony	parallel	cartouche
nilometer		mallet	
counterweight		anvil	
caravan		papyrus	
expedition		artisan	
		magnitude	

YOU RULE: THE GEOGRAPHY OF EGYPT

FOR HOMEWORK

STUDENT STUDY GUIDE

pages 11–12

CAST OF CHARACTERS

Harkhuf (HAR-khoof) Egyptian explorer who lived during the reign of King Pepi II

Pepi (PEH-pee) **II** king of Egypt during Dynasty 6; ruled for about 90 years

THEN and **NOW**

In 1970 the Aswan High Dam was built across the Nile 600 miles south of Cairo. The dam prevents floods by trapping water in a reservoir and controlling its release. But the dam also traps 98 percent of the river's rich sediments and prevents them from flowing downstream. There is now serious erosion in the Delta region because of the lack of silt from floods.

CHAPTER SUMMARY

In this chapter students are introduced to Pepi II, a child who ruled Egypt 4,000 years ago. Despite Pepi II's youth, he wielded despotic power in ancient Egypt. The chapter introduces another kind of power: the power of the environment to shape destiny, specifically the power of the Nile River to shape the lives and fortunes of Egyptians.

PERFORMANCE OBJECTIVES

▶ To understand the relationship between the seasonal flooding of the Nile River and the prosperity of Egypt and growth of trade
▶ To understand how the Nile River's natural barriers (Delta, Cataracts) protected Egypt
▶ To comprehend the extent of the powers invested in ancient Egyptian kings

BUILDING BACKGROUND

Students may have seen the impact of floods on TV or experienced a flood firsthand. Discuss what the word *flood* means to students. (Responses will probably focus on damage to property, loss of homes, and even loss of life.) Explain that in ancient Egypt the flooding of the Nile River was a much anticipated event, one that signaled prosperity, not destruction.

WORKING WITH PRIMARY SOURCES

Read aloud the lines from *The Hymn to the Nile* on page 17. Ask: What concerns about the Nile did Egyptians have that might have caused them to sing this hymn? (*They were concerned that there would be too much annual flooding, or not enough.*)

GEOGRAPHY CONNECTION

Place   Distribute copies of the blackline master for Chapter 1. In studying the map and responding to the questions, students will appreciate Egypt's physical features.

READING COMPREHENSION QUESTIONS

1. Was King Pepi the first Egyptian king? How do you know? (*He was King Pepi II, so there was at least one king before him; in fact, there were several.*)
2. Even though he was six years old, what powers did people believe King Pepi had? (*They believed he had the power to negotiate with the gods to make crops grow and the Nile River flow. They also thought he had the power to live forever.*)
3. How did the Nile River help farmers? (*Its floods left behind rich, black soil good for growing crops. The river also provided water to irrigate fields.*)
4. Where did Harkhuf and other traders travel? What did they bring back to Egypt from each place? (*They traveled to Nubia for gold, to Sinai for turquoise, and to Punt for incense.*)

CRITICAL THINKING QUESTIONS

1. How do we know what King Pepi wrote in a letter to Harkhuf, a trader and caravan conductor, 4,000 years ago? (*Harkhuf copied the letter in stone on his tomb.*)

2. Explain why farmers in the Nile River Valley worried every year. (*They worried that the river might flood too much and wipe out their village, or might not do so enough to ensure a good growing season.*)

3. What tools did farmers in the Nile River Valley use? Why were they important? (*Nilometers measured the height of flood waters each season and provided a record of flooding and a way to compare the results of floods from year to year. Shadufs lifted river water into channels so crops could be irrigated.*)

4. Summarize other ways the Nile River "gave life" to Egypt. (*People believed that the water of the Nile could heal sick people. It also provided natural barriers: swamps in the northern Delta and Cataracts in the south.*)

SOCIAL SCIENCES

Science, Technology, and Society   Have students investigate a 2001 Nile flood in Sudan, south of Egypt. Two useful websites are *http://earthobservatory. nasa.gov/Newsroom/NasaNews/2001/200108315141.html* and, for images of the flood, *www.spaceflightnow.com/news/n0109/02nile/*. Students can prepare an illustrated presentation comparing ancient (nilometer) and modern (satellite imaging) flood-monitoring technologies.

READING AND LANGUAGE ARTS

Reading Nonfiction   As students read the chapter, have them mentally compare the three seasons and the climatic conditions of Egypt with the climate in your region. They can do this throughout the book to help them understand what it might have been like to live in ancient Egypt.

Using Language   Have students identify places in the chapter where the authors address the reader directly as "you." Elicit that this style of writing involves the reader in the material discussed in the chapter.

SUPPORTING LEARNING

English Language Learners   Point out the description of farmers planting and tending their fields in the paragraphs on page 17. Have students identify the verbs used (*lifted, creaked, groaned, raised, pivoted, dropped, parched, inched*) and discuss the meaning of each word and what it adds to the description. Have students use the words in original sentences.

Struggling Readers   Have students use the main idea map graphic organizer in the back of this guide, writing *the Nile* in the center and surrounding it with statements about what the Nile meant to ancient Egyptians.

EXTENDING LEARNING

Enrichment   Invite students to prepare an oral presentation comparing and contrasting the Nile and the Mississippi River. Have them analyze each river's length, the direction of its flow, and its delta, and discuss systems of flood control in use today.

Extension   Have groups create and act out a skit about the three seasons for ancient Egyptian farmers: *akhet, peret,* and *shemu.* The skit should include farmers describing activities associated with each season. One student can narrate.

WRITING

Poetry Have students respond to the questions in the last paragraph of the chapter by taking the role of an ancient ruler of Egypt and writing a poem or song to the Nile.

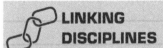

LINKING DISCIPLINES

Science Using print and Internet sources, have students investigate and report on Egypt's oases: What causes them? Who uses them?

NAME   **DATE**

EGYPT: THE NILE AND LANDS BEYOND

Directions

Study the map of ancient Egypt. Then use the map and information from Chapter 1 to answer the questions.

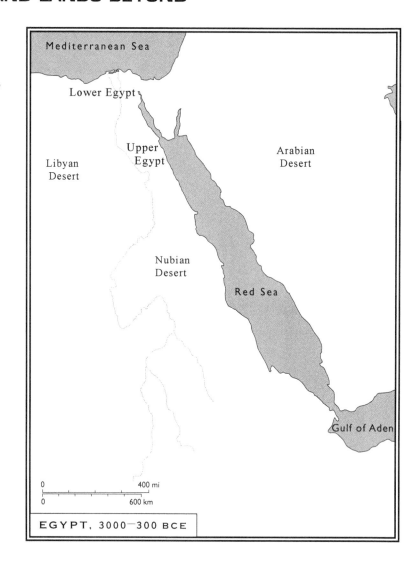

Mediterranean Sea

Lower Egypt

Upper Egypt

Libyan Desert

Arabian Desert

Nubian Desert

Red Sea

Gulf of Aden

0   400 mi

0   600 km

EGYPT, 3000—300 BCE

1. On the map, label the places listed below. Then explain the significance of each of these places to Egyptians of Pepi II's time.

Nile River _____

Nile Delta _____

Cataracts _____

Nubia _____

Sinai _____

2. Explain why ancient Egyptian life centered on the Nile.

_____

_____

NAME _____ **DATE** _____

A. MULTIPLE CHOICE

Circle the letter of the best answer for each question.

1. Without the Nile, Egypt would have been
    a. a great trading nation.
    b. a nation with a great army.
    c. a few wandering bands of nomads.
    d. a wealthy nation.

2. Egyptian farmers eagerly awaited the yearly Nile floods because the floods
    a. brought rich soil to their farms.
    b. allowed farmers to float their crops to market.
    c. brought traders from Punt.
    d. provided water the crops needed to grow.

3. Egypt was protected by all of these natural barriers **except**
    a. cataracts in the Nile to the south.
    b. the swampy Nile delta to the north.
    c. deserts to the east.
    d. mountains to the west.

4. The Egyptian king worked with the gods Hapi and Khnemu to ensure that
    a. harvests were bountiful.
    b. the farmers' cattle would grow fat.
    c. the Nile wasn't too high or too low.
    d. farmers would plant seeds at the right time.

5. The wealth of Egypt depended on its
    a. conquests.
    b. agreements with other countries.
    c. king saying the right prayers.
    d. harvests and trade.

B. SHORT ANSWER

Write one or two sentences to answer each question.

6. How did Egyptian farmers use technology to take advantage of the water of the Nile?

_____

_____

7. Where did Egyptian traders travel, and what riches did they bring back to Egypt?

_____

_____

8. How did the three seasons of Egypt differ from each other?

_____

_____

C. ESSAY

Using details from the chapter, write an essay on a separate sheet of paper describing the benefits and responsibilities of being the king of Egypt.

WRITTEN IN STONE: THE FIRST KING

PAGES 21–26

CAST OF CHARACTERS

Narmer king of Egypt during Dynasty "O"; unified Upper and Lower Egypt

THEN and **NOW**

Hierakonpolis is the modern name of Nekhen, the site where the Palette of Narmer was discovered in 1898. The "Souls of Nekhen," godlike earlier kings, were honored "guests" at later pharaohs' coronations and funerals. Have students write a monologue about King Narmer's accomplishments for his ghost to deliver at a later pharaoh's coronation.

CHAPTER SUMMARY

As the people of ancient Egypt settled down to farm along the Nile, their prosperity led to trade and concentrations of wealth and power. Two villages, Tjeni and Nekhen, grew into large towns with powerful leaders. The chapter focuses on Narmer, believed to be the first king of Egypt, whose exploits and success in uniting Upper and Lower Egypt were commemorated in carvings on a stone called the Palette of Narmer.

PERFORMANCE OBJECTIVES

▶ To understand the connection between agriculture, trade, wealth, and power
▶ To recognize the historical significance of the Palette of Narmer
▶ To interpret ancient Egyptian symbols used on the Palette of Narmer

BUILDING BACKGROUND

Invite students to discuss some beloved American legends: George Washington and the cherry tree, the Pilgrims stepping onto Plymouth Rock, Paul Bunyan and Babe the Blue Ox, Johnny Appleseed. Establish that there is historical truth behind some of the legends and others are wholly made up, but people enjoy them anyway. Explain that ancient Egyptian history includes a legend about its first king that, though carved in stone, may not be entirely true.

WORKING WITH PRIMARY SOURCES

Have students take turns reading aloud portions of the Palette of Narmer description on pages 24–26. Call on volunteers to point out the scenes being described in the illustrations of the Palette.

GEOGRAPHY CONNECTION

Interaction Have students use the map on page 23 to locate Tjeni and Nekhen. Discuss the connection between the location of each town and the wealth and power of the people who lived there.

READING COMPREHENSION QUESTIONS

1. How did people in Tjeni and Nekhen become wealthy? (*Tjeni: controlled traffic on the Nile, was a gateway for traders from the west; Nekhen: close to Nubian gold mines*)
2. What is topsy-turvy about the Nile River? (*It flows from south to north.*)
3. How did the artist who carved the Palette of Narmer show that the king was more important than other people around him? (*The artist made the king larger in relation to the people around him.*)
4. Distribute copies of the blackline master for Chapter 2. Have students use the information in the chapter to create their own versions of the Palette of Narmer.

CRITICAL THINKING QUESTIONS

1. What do *Upper* and *Lower* mean when speaking of Egypt? (*Upper refers to southern Egypt. It is at a higher elevation than northern or Lower Egypt, which is close to sea level.*)

2. Why was the Palette of Narmer created? (*to commemorate King Narmer's unification of Upper and Lower Egypt*)

3. On the Palette of Narmer, what do the bull's tail, bull trampling a foe, and staff symbolize? (*bull's tail and bull symbolize power; staff is symbolic of royalty*)

SOCIAL SCIENCES

Economics   Read aloud the description of *wealthy* in the last paragraph on page 22. Ask students if they agree that "nothing says wealthy like *things*." Then have students pair up and brainstorm a list of possessions that signal a person's wealth and power today. Discuss which items on their list might have been found in the possession of a rich person in Egypt 5,000 years ago.

READING AND LANGUAGE ARTS

Reading Nonfiction   Have students find rhetorical questions—questions that cannot or are not meant to be answered. Point out that the 5,000-year-old Palette of Narmer raises many questions. Ask: How does it make you feel to know there are still things to be discovered about a work of art?

Using Language   This chapter uses vivid adjectives in describing scenes on the Palette of Narmer. Have students find examples of these adjectives and tell how they make the story more interesting.

SUPPORTING LEARNING

English Language Learners   Have students look at the chapter's title and last sentence. Discuss the literal meaning of "written in stone." (The Palette of Narmer is an example.) Discuss what the phrase implies in everyday conversation.

Struggling Readers   Have students use the main idea map graphic organizer in the back of this guide to analyze the Palette of Narmer. Have them write "Palette of Narmer" in the central circle, and headings corresponding to the main images on the Palette in the surrounding circles. Students should then add details from the chapter.

EXTENDING LEARNING

Enrichment   Have students investigate the archaeological excavations at Nekhen (Hierakonpolis) today. An interactive website can be found at *www. archaeology.org/interactive/hierakonpolis/*. Students can prepare a presentation and report back to the class.

Extension   Have a small group of students narrate the story told on the Palette of Narmer and explain the symbols.

WRITING

News Article Ask students to retell the story of the Palette of Narmer in the form of a news article about the king's achievements. Encourage students to incorporate some of the symbolic characters from the Palette in the story— for example the falcon, Horus of Nekhen, protector of the king. Invite them to write headlines for their news stories.

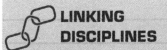

LINKING DISCIPLINES

Art Students can copy scenes or parts of scenes from the Palette of Narmer on one side of large index cards and write explanations of the scenes on the other side.

A NEW PALETTE OF NARMER

Directions

Imagine you are an ancient Egyptian artist who has been asked by the king to carve a palette telling the story of the king's reign. What would you include? In the box below, use the information in Chapter 2 as well as your own imagination to design a new palette for Narmer or for a powerful ruler of Nekhen or Tjeni. Include artwork and symbols that tell

 ▶ the ruler's name.

 ▶ the god who is the ruler's ancestor.

 ▶ how strong the ruler is.

 ▶ what people the ruler has conquered.

 ▶ what great work the ruler has accomplished.

On the sides of the palette, write labels explaining each important element, and draw a line from each label to the part of the picture it describes.

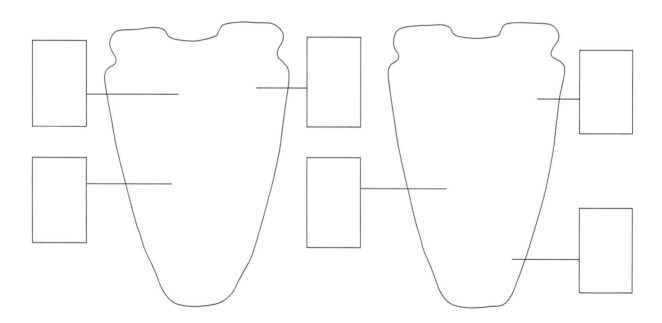

NAME   **DATE**

A. MULTIPLE CHOICE

Circle the letter of the best answer for each question.

1. The early towns of Nekhen and Tjeni grew wealthy because they
   a. were important locations for trade.
   b. had the strongest headsmen.
   c. were close to the Egyptian capital.
   d. had the largest cattle herds.

2. In the towns, artists could make a living because other people
   a. needed artistic things.
   b. would trade things for the artists' talents.
   c. had money.
   d. gave them work on farms.

3. The Palette of Narmer is like a comic book that tells us how King Narmer
   a. defeated the people of Nekhen.
   b. made the gods happy with Egypt.
   c. united Egypt into one kingdom.
   d. felt about the clothes he had to wear.

4. On the palette, King Narmer wears two different hats to show that he is the ruler of
   a. Eastern and Western Egypt.
   b. Egypt and Nubia.
   c. Egypt and Punt.
   d. Upper and Lower Egypt.

5. Some say that, instead of being united by one king, the two lands of Egypt came together
   a. to fight off an invasion.
   b. gradually over generations.
   c. to share their riches.
   d. so they could conquer other kingdoms.

B. SHORT ANSWER

Write one or two sentences to answer each question.

6. What was the land of Egypt like 10,000 years ago?

_____

_____

7. How did the people of Egypt live 6,000 years ago?

_____

_____

8. How was "power born" in the villages of ancient Egypt?

_____

_____

C. ESSAY

Look at the pictures of the Palette of Narmer on pages 24–25 of your book. Using the pictures and the description of the palette in the book, write an essay on a separate sheet of paper discussing the important symbols the artist used.

STAIRWAY TO HEAVEN: THE OLD KINGDOM
PAGES 27–33

CAST OF CHARACTERS

Djoser (ZO-zer) king of Egypt during Dynasty 3; ordered the Step Pyramid to be built

Imhotep (im-HOE-tep) Egyptian architect and physician who designed and built the Step Pyramid for Pharaoh Djoser; worshipped as a god of healing by later Egyptians

THEN and NOW

Excavation of the Step Pyramid complex was the life's work of French scientist Jean-Philippe Lauer (d. 2001). With Cecil Firth, Lauer began investigating the site in the 1920s, continuing through the 20th century. He is credited with uncovering most of what is known about the Step Pyramid. Have students write questions to ask his successors about the site.

CHAPTER SUMMARY

The chapter continues the story of Egypt's growing wealth and power in the era known as the Old Kingdom. King Djoser's Step Pyramid was the first of many pyramids commemorating a king's power and wealth. The fascinating Imhotep, architect of the Step Pyramid, was also a skilled doctor who described treatments for a variety of injuries in the oldest medical document ever found.

PERFORMANCE OBJECTIVES

▶ To relate Egypt's wealth to its agricultural abundance
▶ To understand how the Step Pyramid differed from other royal tombs
▶ To summarize Imhotep's architectural and medical achievements

BUILDING BACKGROUND

Invite students to describe monuments they have seen and admired, either in person or on TV. Discuss how local monuments (to war dead, local dignitaries, or other people or events) achieve their purpose. Explain that in this chapter, students will be reading about a remarkable structure fit to memorialize a king: the first pyramid.

WORKING WITH PRIMARY SOURCES

Encourage students to read more about Imhotep's medical remedies for head wounds online at "Neuroscience for Kids" at *http://faculty.washington.edu/chudler/neurok.html.*

GEOGRAPHY CONNECTION

Location   On a map of ancient Egypt, such as the map at *http://oi.uchicago.edu/OI/INFO/MAP/SITE/Egypt_site_150.dpi.htm*, have students locate Memphis, the capital, and Saqqara, the location of King Djoser's tomb. Have students describe the locations of these two sites. If the map shows latitude, have students compare latitudes with where they live. Ask them to compare climates in their area with climates in Egypt. (*They are close to each other and close to the Nile River and the Nile River Delta, in Lower, or northern, Egypt.*)

READING COMPREHENSION QUESTIONS

1. What do the king's various names tell about what Egyptians believed about the king's powers? (*Many of the king's names connected him with specific gods; Egyptians believed he was divine.*)
2. Why did Egyptians need to get wood from other lands? (*Very few trees grew in Egypt; they needed wood for boats and coffins.*)
3. What did Imhotep build into his design for the Step Pyramid to fool tomb robbers? (*many fake entrances*)
4. Who worked on the Step Pyramid during the flood season? What did they worry about back home? (*Farmers waiting for flood waters to go down; worried about whether there would be enough flood water or too much.*)

5. Copy and distribute the blackline master for Chapter 3 and have students complete the activity using both the text description of the Step Pyramid and the scale drawing of the site.

CRITICAL THINKING QUESTIONS

1. What is the main difference between kingdoms and intermediate periods in Egyptian history? (*Kingdoms were periods of political stability; intermediate periods were times of chaos.*)

2. Compare and contrast the Step Pyramid to earlier designs of royal tombs. (*It rose 200 feet in the air instead of being a hole in the ground covered by a flat stone; it was made of indestructible stone instead of mud bricks that disintegrate over time.*)

3. Draw conclusions about why Imhotep built false entrances into the wall surrounding the burial area. (*Possible answer: to fool grave robbers*)

4. Summarize Imhotep's achievements. (*Design and construction of the Step Pyramid; identifying a variety of ailments and describing treatments for them*)

SOCIAL SCIENCES

Economics Trade in ancient Egypt is described on page 29 as being similar to "trading baseball cards." Have students test their understanding of Egyptian trade by applying the baseball card metaphor to the grain-for-wood trade.

READING AND LANGUAGE ARTS

Reading Nonfiction Have students pick out places in the text where the Step Pyramid is described through King Djoser's eyes. Discuss the effectiveness of this device in helping readers to visualize the scene.

Using Language Have students pick out figurative expressions in the text; for example, *squelching turf wars*, *town with muscle and a headsman with attitude* (page 27), *stairway to heaven* (page 30). Ask students to use the context to explain what these expressions mean.

EXTENDING LEARNING

Enrichment Have students consult print or Internet resources to learn more about Imhotep's extraordinary career as architect, doctor, scribe, and adviser to kings. A useful website is *www.touregypt.net/featurestories/imhotep.htm*. Students can present their findings to the class in an oral report.

Extension Have small groups act out scenes of King Djoser and Imhotep visiting the pyramid construction site.

SUPPORTING LEARNING

Struggling Readers Have students make a three-column chart headed *Dynasties*, *Kingdoms*, and *Intermediate Periods* and complete the chart with details from the chapter.

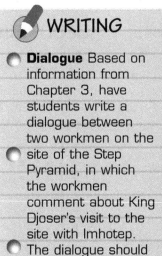

WRITING

Dialogue Based on information from Chapter 3, have students write a dialogue between two workmen on the site of the Step Pyramid, in which the workmen comment about King Djoser's visit to the site with Imhotep. The dialogue should also include comments about job safety and the treatment of on-the-job injuries.

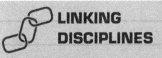

LINKING DISCIPLINES

Health The chapter describes accidents to workers at the Step Pyramid site. Have students investigate modern advice for head injuries at *www. emedicinehealth.com/ fulltext/9339.htm*.

DESCRIBING THE STEP PYRAMID COMPLEX

Directions

On a separate sheet of paper, write a three- or four-paragraph letter from King Djoser to Imhotep, congratulating him on the design of the tomb complex at Saqqara. Use information from Chapter 3 and from the drawings below to supply specific details for King Djoser's comments about the following:

▶ The idea of a pyramid-shaped tomb
▶ The size of the pyramid
▶ The size of the burial complex
▶ The false entrances
▶ The use of stone instead of mud bricks
▶ The optical illusion produced by the entrance columns

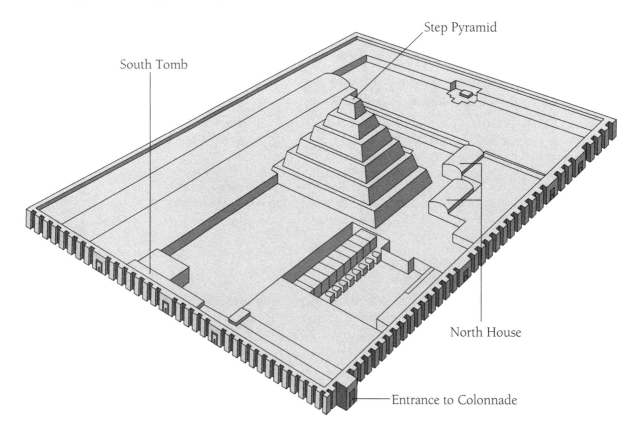

Step Pyramid

South Tomb

North House

Entrance to Colonnade

A. MULTIPLE CHOICE

Circle the letter of the best answer for each question.

1. To truly unify Egypt into one kingdom took several hundred years of
   a. diplomacy.   **c.** trade.
   b. war.   **d.** education.

2. Egypt's wealth was based on the fact that its farmers
   a. were also artists.   **c.** grew new kinds of crops.
   b. also herded cattle.   **d.** grew more food than Egyptians could eat.

3. As Egypt grew richer and more powerful, its king became
   a. like a god.   **c.** hated by other rulers.
   b. trapped in the palace.   **d.** poorer and weaker.

4. King Djoser wanted a special burial tomb built to show the world
   a. the genius of his architect. **c.** what Egyptian peasants could build.
   b. the beautiful stone of Egypt. **d.** how powerful he was.

5. The tomb that Imhotep designed for Djoser was the first tomb made
   a. of bricks.   **c.** for an Egyptian king.
   b. completely of stone.   **d.** during the Old Kingdom.

B. SHORT ANSWER

Write one or two sentences to answer each question.

6. What were the "firsts" involved in building King Djoser's tomb?

   _____

   _____

7. Was working on a pyramid a safe or dangerous job? Explain your answer.

   _____

   _____

8. How do we know that the Egyptian people probably had good harvests during the time Imhotep was building King Djoser's tomb?

   _____

   _____

C. ESSAY

In order to design and build King Djoser's tomb, Imhotep had to be more than just a good architect. Using details from the chapter, write an essay on a separate sheet of paper that draws conclusions about Imhotep's personality and abilities.

CHAPTER 4

THANK *YOU*, ROSETTA STONE: HIEROGLYPHS

PAGES 34–40

FOR HOMEWORK

STUDENT STUDY GUIDE

pages 17–18

CAST OF CHARACTERS

Ptolemy (TALL-uh-mee) **V** Greek king of Egypt best known for the Rosetta Stone, which was inscribed and displayed during his reign

VOCABULARY

hieroglyphs Greek name (meaning "sacred carving") for Egyptian writing symbols because the Greeks saw them carved into the walls of temples and other sacred places

demotic Egyptian cursive writing used for economic and literary documents. **Hieretic** script was used for religious documents.

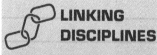

LINKING DISCIPLINES

Art Have students draw their own variations of some of the hieroglyphs from the illustrations in Chapter 4.

CHAPTER SUMMARY

The discovery of the Rosetta Stone by Napoleon's troops in 1799 was the first step in the long, painstaking process of unlocking the secrets of Egyptian hieroglyphs. This chapter explains hieroglyphs, the arduous training required to become an Egyptian scribe, and the challenge of decoding the Rosetta Stone.

PERFORMANCE OBJECTIVES

▶ To understand what hieroglyphs are and how we came to understand their meaning
▶ To recognize hieroglyphs and read some translations of hieroglyphic inscriptions
▶ To describe the intensive training required to become a scribe

BUILDING BACKGROUND

On the board, write an instruction for students, leaving out punctuation and vowels—for example: *Wlcm clss pls dcd ths sntnc* (Welcome, class, please decode this sentence). Challenge students to decode the sentence. Explain that Egyptian writing used pictures for words and sounds and had no vowels or punctuation. Point out that in this chapter they will learn about the giant decoding device that enabled scholars to read Egyptian writing.

WORKING WITH PRIMARY SOURCES

Have students locate places in Chapter 4 (pages 37 and 40) where ancient Egyptians express their feelings about the art of writing hieroglyphs. Then have students search other print and Internet sources for more comments about Egyptians' love of writing.

GEOGRAPHY CONNECTION

Location   On a map of ancient Egypt, such as the map at *http://oi.uchicago. edu/OI/INFO/MAP/SITE/Egypt_site_150dpi.html*, have students locate Abydos, where some of the earliest writing in the world has been found.

READING COMPREHENSION QUESTIONS

1. Why is the Rosetta Stone so important to our understanding of ancient Egypt? (*It made it possible for scholars to translate Egyptian hieroglyphs.*)
2. Why were hieroglyphs hard to understand? (*They were pictures standing for sounds or words, written without punctuation or vowels, and read right to left, left to right, or top to bottom.*)
3. How many ancient Egyptians could read? (*only 1 percent of the population*)
4. What was written on the Rosetta Stone? (*It was a thank-you note from grateful priests to King Ptolemy V, written in three languages.*)

CRITICAL THINKING QUESTIONS

1. Why was Egyptian writing called "sacred carving" by the Greeks? (*because the writing was found carved on the walls of temples and tombs*)
2. What is papyrus and what was it used for? (*Papyrus is a reed that can be used to make paper; scribes wrote on papyrus.*)
3. Scribes played an important role in ancient Egypt. What were some of their writing jobs? (*personal letters, military secrets, magic spells, calculations, birth and death records*)
4. What does the following quote tell you about the position of scribes: "Be a scribe! Your body will be sleek, your hand will be soft." (*Scribes could live well without having to do hard physical labor.*)

SOCIAL SCIENCES

Science, Technology, and Society   Have students identify the various duties of scribes described in Chapter 4. Many of their tasks would be considered technical writing. Challenge students to learn what types of tasks technical writers are called on to do today by reading about technical writing as an occupation or by checking the website of the Society for Technical Communication, *www.stc.org/interestedTC.asp#1*.

READING AND LANGUAGE ARTS

Reading Nonfiction   Point out the process description on page 38 (making paper from papyrus). Discuss the verbs that help the reader visualize what is being described: *peel, slice, covered, pounded, oozed, glued.*

Using Language   Review with students the saying about "death and taxes" on page 34. Check their understanding by asking them to explain why the authors say "it was fitting" that some of the earliest writings were tax records found in a cemetery.

SUPPORTING LEARNING

English Language Learners   Have students read sections of the text to partners. Have partners ask each other questions to review the material.

Struggling Readers   Have students make a sequence chart of the events in the "life" of the Rosetta Stone, from its original purpose to its final deciphering. They can use the sequence of events chart at the back of this guide.

EXTENDING LEARNING

Enrichment   Invite students to find out more about Jean-François Champollion's translation of the Rosetta Stone and report back to the class. Students can find useful information at the BBC Egypt website listed in the Websites section (pages 182–183) at the back of their textbook.

Extension   Distribute copies of the blackline master for Chapter 4. Students can experience what it is like to write hieroglyphs by using a chart equating hieroglyphs to English letters.

WRITING

- **Explanation** Invite students to write a paragraph describing a process with which they are familiar, such as making a sandwich, tying a shoe, opening a can, or sending e-mail. As a model, use the description of making paper from papyrus on page 38.

THEN and NOW

The British Museum has exhibited the Rosetta Stone since 1802, with only one interruption. During World War I, the Rosetta Stone was removed from the museum for safekeeping. Along with other valuable objects, the Rosetta Stone was kept 50 feet underground in a London subway station for two years. Have students write from the Rosetta Stone's point of view a diary entry about its experience in wartime London.

NAME **DATE**

YOUR NAME IN HIEROGLYPHS

Directions

Translate your name into hieroglyphs using the drawings that correspond to the sounds in your name. These hieroglyphs are read left to right (toward the faces of the drawings). Some of the hieroglyphs on this page correspond to vowels to make the words pronounceable.

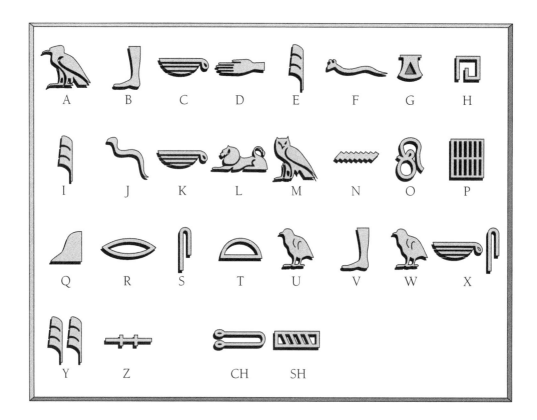

1. Memorize the hieroglyphs for your name and the name of a friend. Test your memory. (Imagine being a scribe and having to memorize more than 700 hieroglyphs!)

2. Use hieroglyphs to write one of these names from the book: *Narmer, Aha, Imhotep, Pepi.* Challenge other students to read it.

_____

_____

NAME   **DATE**

A. MULTIPLE CHOICE

Circle the letter of the best answer for each question.

1. Egyptian hieroglyphs are symbols that stand for
   a. letters.   **c.** ideas or sounds.
   b. sentences.   **d.** religious beliefs.

2. To Egyptians, a word that was written down could
   a. be forgotten.   **c.** change its meaning.
   b. come to life.   **d.** be used for counting.

3. Scribes were important in ancient Egypt because
   a. so few Egyptians could write.   **c.** they trained to be priests.
   b. their education took years.   **d.** they paid taxes.

4. Hieretic writing was a shorthand way of writing hieroglyphs that was used for
   a. religious writing.   **c.** writing everyday documents.
   b. interpreting dreams.   **d.** communication with foreigners.

5. The Rosetta Stone was the key to the ancient Egyptian language because its carvings are in
   a. Greek, Latin, and hieroglyphs.   **c.** Latin, demotic, and hieroglyphs.
   b. Greek, English, and hieroglyphs. **d.** Greek, demotic, and hieroglyphs.

B. SHORT ANSWER

Write one or two sentences to answer each question.

6. Why were scribes such important people in ancient Egypt?

_____

_____

7. Why was being a scribe a desirable job for a young Egyptian?

_____

_____

8. Who were the main translators of the Rosetta Stone? What did each one contribute to translating the stone?

_____

_____

C. ESSAY

Write an essay on a separate sheet of paper describing how Egyptian hieroglyphs developed into a written language.

LIFE IN THE OLD KINGDOM

PAGES 41–63

UNIT OBJECTIVES

In Unit 2, which covers the Old Kingdom Period, 2700–2504 BCE, students encounter several of the most recognizable artifacts of ancient Egypt: animal-headed gods, mummies, and the Great Pyramid. In this unit your students will learn about

- ▶ Egyptian gods who control all aspects of life and the afterlife.
- ▶ Egyptian beliefs about the proper preparation of the dead for the afterlife.
- ▶ the purpose and construction of the Great Pyramid complex at Giza.

PRIMARY SOURCES

Unit 2 includes pictures of artifacts/excerpts from the following primary sources:

- ▶ Great Abydos Stela
- ▶ Plutarch, *Of Isis and Osiris*
- ▶ Pyramid Texts
- ▶ *Book of the Dead*
- ▶ Herodotus, *The Histories*
- ▶ Turin Papyrus
- ▶ Graffiti inside Menkaure's pyramid
- ▶ Dream Stela

BIG IDEAS IN UNIT 2

Religion and **power** are the big ideas in Unit 2. Religion in Egypt centered on the many gods who oversaw daily life and determined where the spirits of the dead would spend the afterlife. Royal power depended on the good will of the gods, which in turn depended on the king's relationship with the priests who tended the shrines of powerful gods. Religion dictated the preparation of bodies of people (and animals) for the afterlife, as well as the design of a king's eternal home—most notably the Great Pyramid at Giza.

You may want to introduce these ideas by eliciting what students know about Egyptian burial practices—mummies and pyramids. Explain that in these chapters they will start to uncover the truth behind myths (such as those found in movies). In reality, Egyptians of all classes, not just kings and queens, invested much time and effort into assuring a positive afterlife for themselves and their pets.

Giza and Saqqara, mentioned in Unit 2, are located along the northern Nile; Abydos is farther south in what was southern or Upper Egypt. Students can locate these sites using a reference such as *Cultural Atlas of Ancient Egypt,* by John Baines and Jaromír Málek (Facts on File Publications, 2000), which includes detailed maps of ancient sites along the Nile as well as information about important sites.

TIMELINE

2700 BCE	Old Kingdom Period begins
2650–2500 BCE	Pyramid age (construction of three major pyramids at Giza) begins
2589–2566 BCE	Khufu (Cheops) rules; builds Great Pyramid at Giza
2558–2532 BCE	Sphinx at Giza built
2532–2504 BCE	Menkaure (Mycerinus) rules, builds Third Pyramid at Giza

UNIT PROJECTS

Cards of the Gods

Have students create a classroom deck of cards for the important Egyptian gods. Partners can investigate the most important Egyptian gods. Each pair can examine one god and learn about his or her origins and powers. Students can copy pictures of the gods onto the front of large index cards and write facts about them on the back. Have partners orally share their cards with the class.

Ramesses I's Mummy Returns

Have students investigate and report on the return of Ramesses I's mummy to Egypt. Students can find a news account at *www.cnn.com/2003/WORLD/meast/ 10/26/mummy.returns.ap/.* They can expand this to consider the question of returning other ancient Egyptian artifacts to Egypt, making a chart showing arguments in favor and against.

Monument Design

Encourage students to design a funerary monument honoring the hero of their choice. The person should be dead and may already have a monument (such as the Washington Monument or the Lincoln Memorial in Washington, D.C.). Have students "think big" and include suggestions for inscriptions that might accompany the monument and honor the person they have chosen.

Build a Model of the Great Pyramid

Interested students can print out a template and build a model of the Great Pyramid from this PBS website: *www.pbs.org/wgbh/nova/pyramid/geometry/ print.html.*

Pyramid Physics

Have a group of students investigate how massive limestone blocks were moved, as described in Chapter 7 and in other sources. Students can draw diagrams explaining the various methods of moving heavy stones to build the pyramids.

ADDITIONAL ASSESSMENT

For Unit 2, divide the class into small research groups and have all students undertake the Cards of the Gods project so you can assess their understanding of the Egyptian gods and their roles in Egyptian life. Use the scoring rubric at the back of this guide to assess students' work, and have students rate their own work with the self-assessment rubric.

LITERATURE CONNECTION

A complete synopsis and translation of The Book of the Dead can be found online at: *www.touregypt.net/bkofdead.htm.* There is an entire website devoted to the Pyramid Texts, which can be a useful resource: *www.pyramidtexts.com.* For a literature activity, divide the class into small groups. Print out some excerpts from either of these sites and distribute copies to the groups. Have students discuss what they think the texts mean, and then have them work together to rephrase the texts in contemporary English. Invite the groups to read their work aloud to the class.

UNIVERSAL ACCESS

The following strategies are designed to cover a range of learning styles and reading, language, and skill levels.

Reading Strategies

▶ Have students use a K-W-L chart to assist them in their reading. Preview each chapter and have students fill in the first column of the chart with what they *know* about the subject. Have them write what they *want to know* about the subject in the second column. When they are finished with the chapter, have them complete the third column by writing what they *learned.*

▶ Point out the Archaeologist at Work feature on pages 48–49 and discuss the convention of using different styles of type to indicate questions and answers. Have students read the interview aloud, taking turns asking and answering the questions. Discuss what the interview adds to the book and why it might have been placed in Chapter 5.

▶ Have groups of three students read this unit, one chapter per student. Each group member should take notes on the reading. Group members can come together to tell each other what they learned about Egyptian gods, mummies, and pyramids.

Writing Strategies

▶ Have partners make a two-column chart with headings for each of the unit's big ideas. Partners should get together after reading each chapter to jot down their observations in each category.

▶ Have students create a visitors' guide to the Great Pyramid, containing factual data, a verbal description, a history of its construction, and information about how to get there and when to visit. They can use information from the chapter and from online resources.

Listening and Speaking Strategies

▶ To spark students' interest, read aloud the title and first paragraph of each chapter. Use the reading as a springboard for predicting what the chapter is about. Record and review students' predictions. When students have finished reading the chapter, ask whether their predictions were correct.

▶ Encourage a group of students to prepare a dramatic reading of a section of a chapter or of an extract from one of the primary sources used in the chapter. They might use props and/or actions to help dramatize the events. The group can present their dramatization to the class.

UNIT VOCABULARY LIST

The following words that appear in Unit 2 are important for your students' understanding of the social studies content as well as for development of literacy. Use these words for vocabulary study or to reinforce language arts skills (e.g., synonyms, compound words, prefixes and suffixes, and related words). The words are listed below in the order in which they appear in the chapters.

Chapter 5	Chapter 6	Chapter 7
shrine	afterlife	disembark
stela	festering	swagger
navigate	meander	plateau
exquisitely	immortality	restlessness
ma'at	deceased	trafficked
sanctuary	essential	lever
ritual	fluids	constellation
mortuary	embalmer	orientation
		overseer
		erosion
		haunch

FOR HOMEWORK

STUDENT STUDY GUIDE

pages 19–20

CAST OF CHARACTERS

Neferhotep (nef-er-HOE-tep) I king of Egypt during Dynasty 13

Plutarch (PLOO-tark) Greek philosopher and biographer

THEN and NOW

Students can visit ancient Egypt via the British Museum at *www. ancientegypt.co.uk/menu. html.* At this concise, well-designed site, recommended on the website section of their book, students can find information on Egyptian gods, geography, mummification, pharaohs, pyramids, and more.

CHAPTER SUMMARY

The gods of Egypt were part of everyday life—the sun's rise, the Nile's floods, and even more mundane aspects. The job of the pharaohs was to make sure the gods were happy. Peace among the gods maintained *ma'at*, the precious balance on which Egypt's own peace and prosperity depended.

PERFORMANCE OBJECTIVES

▶ To identify some of the Egyptian gods and the powers they wielded
▶ To describe the pharaoh's and the priests' duties in keeping the gods happy
▶ To understand what the stories of Osiris, Isis, Seth, and Horus meant to Egyptians

BUILDING BACKGROUND

Read aloud the words from the last paragraph on page 47: "For Egyptians, the stories about the gods were comforting and provided guidance . . . " Invite students to keep the words *comfort* and *guidance* in mind as they read stories about the gods in this chapter.

WORKING WITH PRIMARY SOURCES

Have different groups act out scenes from Plutarch's Osiris and Isis stories. For example, a group can act out the description of Seth tricking Osiris into climbing into his custom-made coffin (pages 44–45) while one student narrates.

GEOGRAPHY CONNECTION

Location Have students locate Saqqara and Abydos on a map of ancient Egypt such as the map at *http://oi.uchicago.edu/OI/INFO/MAP/SITE/ Egypt_site_150dpi.html.* Ask: Why do you think important sites were located close to the Nile? (*Ease of transportation of people, animals, and building materials.*) Ask students to give an example from the chapter of the Nile's being used as transportation. (*King Neferhotep asked for the statue of Osiris to be brought to his barge on the Nile when he traveled to Abydos.*)

READING COMPREHENSION QUESTIONS

1. What form did Egyptian gods take—human or animal? (*Some were human, some animal, and some were both.*)
2. Who was the most important god in ancient Egypt? Why? (*The sun god was most important, because he made the sun rise every day.*)
3. How did King Neferhotep investigate the care of Osiris's spirit? (*He read the ancient texts that explained how to care for the god's statue.*)
4. How did Isis recover Osiris's body after Seth killed him? (*She and her sister sailed in a boat through the marshes collecting pieces of Osiris and sewed him back together.*)
5. Distribute copies of the blackline master for Chapter 5. Have students complete the activity to help them understand the characteristics of the gods, particularly Osiris, Isis, Seth, and Horus.

CRITICAL THINKING QUESTIONS

1. Summarize why it was important to King Neferhotep that the god Osiris be well taken care of. (*Keeping the gods happy was the job of the king. When the gods were happy, life in Egypt was in balance [*ma'at*].*)

2. Infer why ordinary people lined the route when the statue of Osiris was taken to meet King Neferhotep. (*This was their chance to see the statue of Osiris, their most important god. Only priests went into the temple where it was kept.*)

3. What are some of the reasons a king had 14 boats buried with him at Abydos? (*possibly to deliver supplies to him in the afterlife or to allow him to sail through the world of the dead*)

4. What did ancient Egyptians believe about Horus? (*They believed that one day he would defeat Seth completely and then all sorrow would end.*)

SOCIAL SCIENCES

Civics   Discuss the various responsibilities of King Neferhotep described in this chapter. Ask: Why was it important to him that Osiris be well cared for?

READING AND LANGUAGE ARTS

Reading Nonfiction   The chapter contains a two-page interview with archaeologist David O'Connor. Have students consider why the interview appears in this chapter. (*It describes excavations at Abydos, location of Osiris's shrine.*) Ask: What does a primary source like the interview provide that a straight narrative does not? (*Professor O'Connor answers in his own words.*) After students read the interview, have them articulate questions they would like to ask Professor O'Connor.

Using Language   Have students use a dictionary to discover the etymology of *archaeology* (from the Greek *archaio-* + *-logia*, or "ancient science"). Elicit that archaeology is the scientific study of ancient humans. Have students list and define related words (*archaeologist, archaeological, archaeologically*) and use them in sentences.

SUPPORTING LEARNING

English Language Learners   Review with students the pronunciation of the names of the gods who appear in this chapter.

Struggling Readers   Have students paraphrase the legend of Osiris (pages 44–45) and read it aloud to a small group.

EXTENDING LEARNING

Enrichment   Have a group of students use online resources to find out about the current status of excavations at Abydos, particularly Osiris's boats. For current news related to Egyptian antiquities, students can go to *www.touregypt.net/egyptnews.htm*, recommended in the website listings of their book.

Extension   Invite students to create a comic book version of a scene of conflict among the gods described in the chapter, such as Horus fighting Seth, who has himself turned into a ferocious crocodile (page 45). Stick figures, narrative boxes, and speech bubbles can be used to tell the story in a series of panels.

WRITING

Letter Have students write a letter from King Neferhotep to the priests of Osiris explaining why he wants to examine the "ancient writings." In the letter, students should show that they understand the importance of maintaining *ma'at* in Egypt.

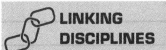

LINKING DISCIPLINES

Art Invite students to choose one of the gods from the list on page 46 and use books or online sources to find a picture of the god. They can then draw their own picture of that god, label it with the god's attributes, and display it in class.

NAME   **DATE**

EGYPTIAN GODS' FAMILY TREE

Directions

Using what you read in Chapter 5, add information about Osiris, Isis, Seth, and Horus to the "family tree" below. Use complete sentences to summarize the conflict between Osiris and Seth and explain how Horus restored *ma'at* to Egypt.

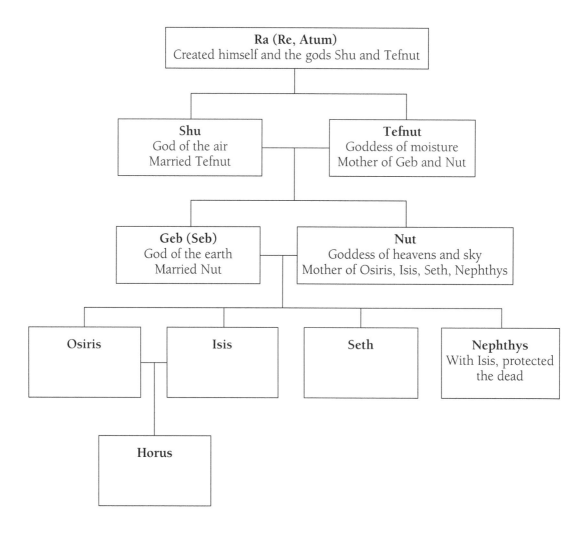

NAME _____ **DATE** _____

A. MULTIPLE CHOICE

Circle the letter of the best answer for each question.

1. The ancient Egyptians had a god for
   a. everything.
   b. natural objects only.
   c. dead relatives only.
   d. protection against good gods.

2. The Egyptians believed that if their gods were unhappy, their lives would be
   a. unaffected.
   b. unsettled and dangerous.
   c. peaceful and prosperous.
   d. much improved.

3. The battle between Seth and Horus was
   a. a fight between chaos and happiness.
   b. over a beautiful goddess.
   c. a family feud between uncle and nephew.
   d. of no interest to humans.

4. Inside the temples, priests cared for the gods by
   a. leading the people in prayers.
   b. bathing and feeding the gods' statues.
   c. drawing pictures of the gods.
   d. retelling stories of the gods.

5. To Egyptians, stories about the gods were
   a. used as bedtime stories.
   b. intended to make children behave well.
   c. provided guidance in an unpredictable world.
   d. changed each time a new pharaoh took the throne.

B. SHORT ANSWER

Write one or two sentences to answer each question.

6. Explain your opinion of why the sun god was the most important Egyptian god.

_____

_____

7. What would make the Egyptians think that life was not in balance?

_____

_____

8. What did Egyptian priests have to do to purify themselves?

_____

_____

C. ESSAY

Write an essay on a separate sheet of paper explaining this statement: *One of the pharaoh's most important jobs was to take care of the gods.* **Use details from the chapter to support the main idea. Include information about what the job included as well as why it was important.**

IT'S A WRAP: MUMMIES AND THE AFTERLIFE PAGES 50–56

THEN and NOW

A mummy, believed to be the remains of Ramesses I, was returned to Egypt in 2003 by a museum in Atlanta, Georgia. The mummy had been purchased from a Canadian museum three years earlier and was probably taken out of Egypt in the 1860s. Ramesses I was the first pharaoh of the 19th Dynasty, which included Ramesses II and Ramesses III. Ask students to list reasons they feel this return was a good idea or a bad idea.

 VOCABULARY

mummification from *mummiya* (pitch) because bodies preserved by mummification appeared to have been dipped in pitch, which comes from tar

CHAPTER SUMMARY

In Egypt religious beliefs dictated treatment of the dead. Mummifying a dead person (or sacred animal or beloved pet) kept the body intact and assured a peaceful afterlife in the Field of Reeds. The "recipes" for preparing a mummy were highly prized secrets of embalmers that varied over the centuries and with the social class of the dead person.

PERFORMANCE OBJECTIVES

- ▶ To understand the religious rationale behind Egyptians' mummifying the dead
- ▶ To describe the tests a person's spirit had to go through to reach the Field of Reeds
- ▶ To summarize the steps in preparing a mummy

BUILDING BACKGROUND

Ask students what they associate with Egyptian mummies. Clarify any misunderstanding, such as the belief that only kings and queens were mummified. Explain that many types of people had their bodies mummified to ensure a peaceful afterlife. Explain that scientists have studied mummies carefully and that this chapter will explain how and why bodies were mummified.

WORKING WITH PRIMARY SOURCES

Discuss with students the purpose of The Book of the Dead and the relevance of the quotes on page 52 to that purpose. Suggest that interested students read more excerpts from The Book of the Dead at *www.touregypt.net/bkofdead.htm*. This website is recommended in the Websites section of their book.

GEOGRAPHY CONNECTION

Place   Have students locate Tuna el-Gebel on a map of Egypt and read more about the cemetery of Hermopolis, where millions of ibis mummies (used as religious offerings) have been found. Have them work together in class to describe the location, its climate, its position in relation to other locations, and other aspects of the place.

READING COMPREHENSION QUESTIONS

1. What did the Field of Reeds mean to the ancient Egyptians? (*The Field of Reeds was the afterlife, where there was no illness, plenty of food, and where no one had to work.*)
2. Why was the body of a person who died important to the ancient Egyptians? (*The spirit of a dead person would not be able to get to the Field of Reeds without a body.*)
3. How do we know the recipe for making a mummy? (*from the writings of the Greek historians Herodotus and Diodorus Siculus*)

4. Why were animals mummified in ancient Egypt? (*Sacred animals and beloved pets were preserved after death so that their spirits could go to the Field of Reeds.*)

CRITICAL THINKING QUESTIONS

1. Compare and contrast natural mummification with mummification by embalmers. (*Mummification in the sand was much simpler than mummification by embalming. In natural mummification people were buried in the hot, dry desert sand, which dried out and preserved the body. Embalmers removed a body's organs [except the heart] and dried the body with natron for 40 days. Then the body was stuffed and wrapped. Embalmers chanted spells, and the dead person's family collected cloth for wrapping the mummy.*)

2. What was the purpose of the Book of the Dead, the Pyramid Texts, and the Coffin Texts? (*to guarantee that a person's spirits could pass through the labyrinth of portals into the hall of judgment*)

3. Refer students to the excerpt from the Book of the Dead, "The Negative Confession," in *The World in Ancient Times Primary Sources and Reference Volume* for examples of what people on their way to the afterlife were supposed to say to the gods who questioned them.

SOCIAL SCIENCES

Science, Technology, and Society   Distribute copies of the blackline master for Chapter 6 so students can review the stages in the process of making a mummy.

READING AND LANGUAGE ARTS

Reading Nonfiction   Have students identify the ways the text indicates the steps in making a mummy (pages 55–56): "First stop . . . Next stop . . . From start to finish . . . And that's a wrap."

Using Language   Remind students that in English, proper nouns, such as the names of people, countries, wars, battles, rivers, and places, are capitalized. Assign small groups a section of the chapter, then have them list the proper nouns they find and sort them into categories.

SUPPORTING LEARNING

English Language Learners   Have students tell the difference between *spells*, *scrolls*, and *texts* as discussed in the chapter.

Struggling Readers   Have students make a chart summarizing the steps a spirit had to take to gain entrance into the Field of Reeds.

EXTENDING LEARNING

Enrichment   Have students find out more about the techniques used to establish the age of a mummy. They can report their findings to the class.

Extension   Ask a group of students to find out more about mummies by visiting the Cleveland Museum of Art website at *www.clevelandart.org/kids/egypt/rosefaq.html*. They can report back to the class what they learn.

 **WRITING**

Explanation Have students write a letter from the point of view of an ancient Egyptian to the editor of the imaginary *Daily Egyptian News* explaining why mummification of your animals is important to you.

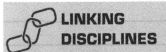 **LINKING DISCIPLINES**

Physical Science Encourage students to investigate how heat removes moisture from matter, such as apple slices. They can weigh apple slices before and after exposing them to hot, dry air and connect the results to the statements on page 54 concerning natural mummification of bodies buried in desert sand.

NAME _____   **DATE** _____

MAKING A MUMMY

Directions

Using what you read in the chapter, fill in the three boxes with information about each stage in preparing a mummy. On the lines below each box, summarize the reasons for each step.

Step 1—*Ibu*, Place of Washing

_____
_____
_____
_____
_____
_____

Reasons for Step 1

_____
_____

Step 2—*Per-nefer*, House of Mummification

_____
_____
_____
_____
_____
_____

Reasons for Step 2

_____
_____

Step 3—*Wabet*, House of Purification

_____
_____
_____
_____
_____
_____

Reasons for Step 3

_____
_____

NAME _____ **DATE** _____

A. MULTIPLE CHOICE

Circle the letter of the best answer for each question.

1. Which of the following is **not** one of the tests ancient Egyptians had to pass in order to get into the Field of Reeds after death?
   a. respond to challenges in order to pass through a labyrinth
   b. sing a song to the Lord of the Mummy Wrappings
   c. declare their innocence to 42 gods
   d. have their heart weighed against a feather

2. The Pyramid Texts was a book of spells buried with pharaohs so that they could
   a. know what to do in the afterlife.
   b. talk to living people.
   c. protect themselves from danger.
   d. answer questions of the gatekeepers.

3. In the beginning, bodies were preserved by being buried in
   a. the sand.
   b. a coffin.
   c. the Nile.
   d. a brick tomb.

4. The importance of mummification is best explained by which statement?
   a. It provided embalmers a chance to practice their arts.
   b. It prevented decay.
   c. It preserved a person's brain.
   d. It preserved the body so the person's spirits could enter the Field of Reeds.

5. Before mummification, the Egyptians removed all of the organs of the body except the heart because it was believed to be
   a. the location of the soul.
   b. sacred to the god Anubis.
   c. the most important organ in the body.
   d. the key to the Field of Reeds.

B. SHORT ANSWER

Write one or two sentences to answer each question.

6. What did Egyptians think their afterlife in the Field of Reeds would be like?
   _____
   _____

7. Describe the god Anubis and the final test he gave to spirits.
   _____
   _____

8. What purpose did the Pyramid Texts, the Coffin Texts, and the Book of the Dead have in common?
   _____
   _____

C. ESSAY

Use information from the chapter to write an essay on a separate sheet of paper describing the body's three spirits and their roles after death.

CHAPTER 7

TOMB BUILDERS: THE PYRAMID AGE/ THE OLD KINGDOM   PAGES 57–63

CAST OF CHARACTERS

Khufu (COO-foo) king of Egypt (known to the Greeks as Cheops) who built the Great Pyramid, the first of three large pyramids at Giza

Thutmose (TUT-moze) **IV** king of Egypt who ordered the Dream Stela inscribed to record a dream he had while sleeping between the paws of the Great Sphinx at Giza

THEN and **NOW**

Excavations at Giza continue to uncover ancient structures and artifacts. In 2004 the director of Egypt's Supreme Council of Antiquities announced the discovery of a 2,500-year-old tomb hidden 33 feet below ground between one of the pyramids at Giza and the Sphinx.

CHAPTER SUMMARY

The Sphinx and the Great Pyramid at Giza are two of the most widely recognized symbols of ancient Egypt. The focus in this chapter is on the workers who built the Great Pyramid and the techniques by which they created that towering monument to King Khufu. At the end of the chapter, the Sphinx's story is also touched on.

PERFORMANCE OBJECTIVES

▶ To understand the positioning and construction of the Great Pyramid
▶ To summarize the contributions of the thousands of workers who built the pyramids
▶ To describe the Sphinx and understand its mythical power in Egyptian history

BUILDING BACKGROUND

Challenge students to name one or more of the tallest buildings in the world today. Explain that they are going to read about a structure that for 4,000 years was the tallest structure in the world: the Great Pyramid.

WORKING WITH PRIMARY SOURCES

Invite a small group of students to find out more about the graffiti written on tombs to discourage tomb robbers.

GEOGRAPHY CONNECTION

Location   Ask students to define "true north" and explain the significance of the modern discovery that the Great Pyramid is less than a tenth of a degree off true north (page 60).

READING COMPREHENSION QUESTIONS

1. Why did the king's men come on barges to villages along the Nile during the flood time? (*to collect workers to work on the pyramids*)
2. Why did many farmers work on the pyramids during flood season? (*because when their fields were underwater, farmers were available to do other types of work*)
3. Why did King Khufu need boats in his tomb? (*They would carry his spirit to the stars.*)
4. How was the Sphinx preserved over thousands of years? (*It was buried in sand.*)
5. Distribute copies of the blackline master for Chapter 7 so students can better understand the importance of the Great Pyramid.

CRITICAL THINKING QUESTIONS

1. Describe two ways in which the workers building the pyramids used water. (*Wooden wedges were driven into stone in the quarry and then soaked with water to make them swell, splitting the stone. Water was used to create mud on tracks to slide limestone blocks.*)

2. What bargain did the Sphinx make with Prince Thutmose? (*If Thutmose would clear away the sand from around the Sphinx, the Sphinx would make him king.*)

3. Answer the question posed on page 59: How would you have felt that first day at Giza? (*Students' responses should show they understand the massive scope of the project, the number of people and effort involved in building the Great Pyramid, and a feeling of privilege at working on such an important project for the king.*)

SOCIAL SCIENCES

Science, Technology, and Society Ask students to create a sequence chart showing the methods workers used to cut, move, and position limestone blocks while building the Great Pyramid.

READING AND LANGUAGE ARTS

Reading Nonfiction Have students take turns reading aloud from the chapter and commenting on the effectiveness of the authors' use of "you" to put readers in the scenes being described.

Using Language Read aloud the second paragraph of the chapter, and have students identify the figurative expressions. (*Word . . . rippled from house to mud-brick house; Men and women trickled out . . . ; You caught your breath.*) Call on volunteers to explain their meaning.

SUPPORTING LEARNING

English Language Learners Ask students to explain in their own words what is happening in the picture on page 61.

Struggling Readers Have students use the main idea map graphic organizer in the back of this guide. Have them write *Great Pyramid* in the middle and surround it with important details from the text.

EXTENDING LEARNING

Enrichment Challenge students to find out where the kings of Egypt lived before they went to their tombs. They can find out about the "palace hypothesis" of archaeologist Mark Lehner by accessing an interview with him at this website: *www.pbs.org/wgbh/nova/pyramid/excavation/palacehypothesis.html.*

Extension Have small groups of students write skits based on scenes in the chapter that are related to the building of the Great Pyramid. The skits should explain who was drafted to work on the Great Pyramid, how awe inspiring it was, and how it was built. Have students perform their skits for the class.

WRITING

Dialogue Write a dialogue between the Sphinx and Prince Thutmose based on information on page 63.

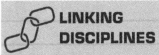

LINKING DISCIPLINES

Math On the blackline master for Chapter 7, have students do the calculations and answer the questions based on the Great Pyramid Facts.

VOCABULARY

Mennefer literally, "eternal beauty"; capital of ancient Egypt during reign of King Khufu, now known as Memphis

mer ancient Egyptian word for *pyramid*

NAME   DATE

BUILDING THE GREAT PYRAMID

Directions

For each activity and item listed, write a brief description of its significance to the construction of the Great Pyramid based on information in the chapter. Use complete sentences.

Activity/Item	Significance to Construction of Great Pyramid
1. King's men shouting out names in the village	
3. Giant baking ovens	
4. Blocks of limestone	
5. Mud-covered tracks	
6. Ramp of stone and rubble	
7. Men pouring water on wooden wedges	
8. True north	

Great Pyramid Facts

Original height: about 482 feet **Base area:** more than 13 acres (nearly 10 football fields) **Length of each side of the base:** 756 feet	**Time to completion:** 23 years **Measurement used in construction:** royal cubit (20.62 inches)

1. If you were to walk around the base of the Great Pyramid, how far would that be?

_____

2. On average, how many feet were added to the height of the pyramid during each year of construction?

_____

3. Workers who were building the tombs, temples, and pyramids had cubit sticks for measuring. Use the information in the box to calculate the height of the Great Pyramid in cubits.

_____

NAME   **DATE**

A. MULTIPLE CHOICE

Circle the letter of the best answer for each question.

1. Which of the following is **not** a method used in working with limestone blocks in building the Great Pyramid?
   a. cut with diamond-toothed saws
   b. trimmed with copper hammers
   c. lifted with ropes and levers
   d. shoved along muddy tracks

2. With which constellation was the Great Pyramid aligned?
   a. Orion
   b. Cassiopeia
   c. Great Bear
   d. Little Bear

3. How many stone blocks were used in building the Great Pyramid?
   a. 1,000,000
   b. 1,230,000
   c. 230,000
   d. 2,300,000

4. The Overseer of All the King's Works was in charge of
   a. the workers' tombs at Giza.
   b. only the workers cutting and moving limestone.
   c. all the workers at the Great Pyramid site.
   d. workers building boats for the king's use in the afterlife.

5. Which statement about the Great Pyramid is still true?
   a. It is the tallest building.
   b. It is taller than the Sphinx.
   c. It is taller than the Eiffel Tower.
   d. It is the oldest tomb in Egypt.

B. SHORT ANSWER

Write a sentence or two to answer each question.

6. How were laborers chosen to work on the pyramids?

_____

_____

7. How did the Egyptians move the stone blocks from the quarry to the pyramid?

_____

_____

8. Why was the orientation of the Great Pyramid critical for the king?

_____

C. ESSAY

On a separate sheet of paper, use details from the chapter to describe the sphinx and its mythical power in Egyptian history.

FROM CHAOS TO GOLDEN AGE

PAGES 64–87

UNIT OBJECTIVES

Unit 3 covers the period 2278–1450 BCE, years during which Egypt experienced times of chaos (the First and Second Intermediate Periods) and times of stability (the Middle and New Kingdoms). In this unit your students will learn

► how power shifted from the king to his governors in the First Intermediate Period.
► why ancient Egypt was renowned for having the best medical care of its time.
► how Egyptians waged war against the invading Hyksos.
► characteristics of the golden age under Queen Hatshepsut and King Thutmose III.

PRIMARY SOURCES

Unit 3 includes pictures of artifacts/excerpts from the following primary sources:

► *Admonitions of Ipuwer*
► Ankhtyfy's tomb inscriptions
► *Dialogue Between a Man Tired of Life and His Ba*
► *The Tale of Sinuhe*
► Homer, the *Odyssey*
► Diodorus Siculus, *Biblioteca Historica*
► Ebers Papyrus
► Herodotus, *The Histories*
► Wall paintings from the Tomb of the Physician
► Edwin Smith Papyrus
► Manetho, *Aegyptiaca*
► Papyrus Sallier 1
► Tomb inscriptions of Ahmose of Ibana
► Josephus Flavius quoting Manetho's *Aegyptiaca*
► Government records
► Inscriptions at Hatshepsut's mortuary temple
► Tomb inscription of an army scribe
► Inscription at Karnak temple

BIG IDEAS IN UNIT 3

Power, conflict, and **medicine** are the big ideas presented in Unit 3. The unit covers rulers who lost or had little power and those who consolidated power in their own hands. After King Pepi II, the last king of the Old Kingdom Period, power shifted to the governors of outlying provinces during the First Intermediate Period. In the Middle Kingdom, centralized power was back in the hands of rulers. But their centralized power was challenged by the Hyksos, invaders who took control of northern Egypt in the Second Intermediate Period. Conflict with the Hyksos resulted in the return of power to Egyptian rulers during the New Kingdom. Two rulers, Queen Hatshepsut and King Thutmose III, exemplify this golden age, in which conflict over control of trade routes was resolved in Egypt's favor. Ancient Egyptian illnesses and treatments—from herbal medicines to brain surgery (with obsidian instruments)—and even malpractice are also discussed in this unit.

Introduce these ideas by eliciting what students know about ancient Egyptian rulers. They may describe kings with absolute power and fabulous wealth. Point out that during the period covered in Unit 3, not everyone with power was a king (at different times provincial governors and one queen also wielded power) or even an Egyptian (the Hyksos invaders ruled part of the country until driven out).

GEOGRAPHY CONNECTION

Refer students to the maps on pages 76 and 86. Have students locate places mentioned in Unit 3 on those maps and on a larger map of ancient Egypt.

TIMELINE

2278–2184 BCE	Reign of Pepi II
2180 BCE	First Intermediate Period
2040 BCE	Middle Kingdom Period begins
1991–1962 BCE	Reign of Amenemhet I
1971–1926 BCE	Reign of Senwosert (Senusret) I
1782 BCE	Hyksos invade; Second Intermediate Period begins
1570 BCE	Hyksos are expelled; New Kingdom begins
1498–1483 BCE	Reign of Hatshepsut
1483–1450 BCE	Reign of Thutmose III
1483 BCE	Thutmose III defeats rebels in Battle of Megiddo

UNIT PROJECTS

Royal Mystery

Invite students to investigate why all traces of Hatshepsut's rule disappeared for 3,000 years after her death. They can gather information from print and online sources, such as *www.bbc.co.uk/history/ancient/egyptians/hatshepsut_01.shtml*, recommended in the Websites section of the student book.

Interviews

Have students imagine they can interview either Pepi II, Seqenenre, Hatshepsut, or Thutmose III about events during their reigns. Organize the class into small groups and have team members pose questions for one person to answer in the role of ruler. Have each group prepare a report on their interview, to present orally to the class.

Thutmose III Goes to War

Invite students to learn more about Thutmose III's actions and decisions leading up to the Battle of Megiddo. Students can find information and a map of Megiddo and surrounding areas online at *www.touregypt.net/featurestories/megiddo.htm*, recommended in the Websites section of the student book.

Hatshepshut Becomes King

Have students investigate different aspects of Hatshepshut's reign to increase their understanding not only of how Hatshepshut solidified her power but of the activities of Egyptian kings. Topics can include Hatshepshut's family tree, how she came to be coruler and then sole ruler, her support by the priests of Amun, the circumstances of her burial, and her mortuary temple. Students can begin their research at *www.touregypt.net/HistoricalEssays/hatshepsut.htm*.

Archaeology: Tell el-Dab'a

Have students investigate and report on archaeological efforts at Tell el-Dab'a to uncover Avaris, the Hyksos capital in the Nile Delta. Students can find information online at *www.touregypt.net/featurestories/niledeltaruins.htm* that will help them locate the site on detailed maps of the region and provide information for a report to the class about discoveries there.

ADDITIONAL ASSESSMENT

For Unit 3, divide the class into groups and have them all undertake the Interviews project so you can assess their understanding of Egyptian trade and the reigns of Egyptian kings. Use the scoring rubric at the back of this guide to assess students' work, and have students rate their own work with the self-assessment rubric.

LITERATURE CONNECTION

The mysteries of ancient Egypt provide a compelling backdrop to many works of historical fiction written by contemporary authors. Students will enjoy reading the following titles. (You might want to advise students that historical fiction is not always accurate in its details.)

► McGraw, Eloise Jarvis. *Mara, Daughter of the Nile*. New York: Puffin Story Books, 1981. The fictional story of a 17-year-old slave girl living under the reign of Hatshepsut

► McGraw, Eloise Jarvis. *The Golden Goblet*. New York: Puffin Newbery Library, 1990. This is the fictional story of an orphan, Ranofer, who finds a golden goblet stolen from the City of the Dead.

UNIVERSAL ACCESS

The following strategies are designed to cover a range of learning styles and reading, language, and skill levels.

Reading Strategies

► To facilitate reading, help students preview the artwork and captions in each chapter to make predictions about the content.

► Call on students to read aloud quotations from the primary sources. Encourage them to make their voices expressive and to use hand gestures where appropriate. Fit the reading passage to the abilities of each student.

► Chapter 9 deals with several subtopics under the general topic of health. Have students create main idea statements for each subtopic. Then have them point out details or examples that support the main ideas.

Writing Strategies

► Have students make an idea web, using the big idea *power* as the central circle. They can fill in the outer circles with details about the power held or lost by different people and groups discussed in this unit.

▶ Use the outline graphic organizer (see the back of this guide) to model how to create an outline for a chapter. Have partners break a chapter into sections, read the section together, and then outline the information.

Listening and Speaking Strategies

▶ Small groups can create a monologue for Queen Hatshepsut, describing the expedition to Punt, or for Ahmose the soldier, describing the battles he fought against the Hyksos. Students should present their monologues to the class, live or through a recording.

▶ Encourage a group of students to prepare a panel presentation—The Hyksos: Pro and Con—in which their contributions to Egypt are weighed against their presence as a foreign power in Egypt.

UNIT VOCABULARY LIST

The following words that appear in Unit 3 are important for your students' understanding of the social studies content as well as for development of literacy. Use these words for vocabulary study or to reinforce language arts skills (e.g., synonyms, compound words, prefixes and suffixes, and related words). The words are listed below in the order in which they appear in the chapters.

Chapter 8	Chapter 9	Chapter 10	Chapter 11
luxurious	salve	vertical	colonnade
conceited	millennia	garrison	transform
climate	barbaric	adapt	divine
bleak	administer	mercenaries	mortal
rigid	accordance	professional	deity
centralized	absolved	besieged	trinket
botanist	malady	gilded	frantic
eternity	physician	siege	vulnerable
draughtsman	prescription		
monarchy	tracheotomy		
anarchy	anesthesia		
	antibiotic		
	dosage		
	draught		
	asthmatic		

FROM MONARCHY TO ANARCHY AND BACK AGAIN
PAGES 64–69

CAST OF CHARACTERS

Pepi (PEH-pee) **II** king of Egypt who ruled for 90 years

Ankhtyfy (AHNK-tee-fee) Egyptian governor and warlord during First Intermediate Period

Senwosert (SEN-whe-sert) king of Egypt

Sinuhe (SIN-oo-way) Egyptian character, possibly fictional; story of his wanderings and life takes place during reigns of Amenemhet and Senwosert

THEN and **NOW**

Evidence found in texts and paintings in temples and tombs shows that ancient Egyptians, like people today, enjoyed jokes, political satire, parodies, and cartoon-like art. Have students find examples of ancient Egyptian humor and report back to the class.

CHAPTER SUMMARY

During the First Intermediate Period, power gradually shifted from the king to provincial governors who recruited their own armies. The result was chaos and bloodshed as well as new freedoms and new ways of thinking. Centralized power returned with the Middle Kingdom.

PERFORMANCE OBJECTIVES

▶ To understand how power shifted during the First Intermediate Period
▶ To describe how the First Intermediate Period was not as bleak as Middle Kingdom writers described it
▶ To see *The Tale of Sinuhe* as a Middle Kingdom story glorifying Egypt

BUILDING BACKGROUND

Ask students what it means for a story to have a "moral." Discuss examples of stories that have morals, such as George Washington chopping down the cherry tree and refusing to lie, or the boy who cried wolf. Explain that in this chapter they will read a story with a moral that inspired Egyptians for centuries.

WORKING WITH PRIMARY SOURCES

Refer students to excerpts from "The Maxims of Ptah-Hotep" in the *World in Ancient Times Primary Sources and Reference Volume* for an idea of how people were expected to behave in the royal court. Invite volunteers to read the excerpts aloud.

GEOGRAPHY CONNECTION

Location   The sidebar on page 64 names cities that were capitals of ancient Egypt. Have students locate the cities on a map of ancient Egypt, describe the locations and why people settled there, then use a map of modern Egypt to determine their names today.

READING COMPREHENSION QUESTIONS

1. How was the shift in power from the king to the governors shown in the homes of the governors? (*The governors built palaces and hired artists to decorate their homes and tombs. Instead of sending local goods to the king, the governors kept them to pay for their rich lifestyles.*)
2. How did the governors use power once they had it? (*They built up armies and fought each other in bloody civil wars.*)
3. Why did rich Egyptians want to get copies of the Coffin Texts? (*Before the First Intermediate Period only kings were assured of an afterlife; with the directions and maps in the Coffin Texts, other Egyptians could have life after death, too.*)
4. In the *Tale of Sinuhe*, what is Sinuhe's wish? Does it come true? (*His wish is to return to Egypt and build his tomb there. Yes, King Senwosert grants his wish and builds a pyramid for his tomb.*)

5. What were some of the new ways Egyptians expressed themselves during the First Intermediate Period? (*Artists used new styles, painting ordinary people at work using new inventions.*)

CRITICAL THINKING QUESTIONS

1. Explain how grain contributed to a shift in power from the king to the provincial governors. (*When governors moved out of the capital city to live in the provinces they governed, goods such as the grain that had been sent to the capital were kept in the provinces and distributed by the governors. This shifted power away from the king.*)

2. Why do you think *The Tale of Sinuhe* was so popular with generations of Egyptians? (*It made them proud to be Egyptians. The story's moral is that Egypt is the best country in the world.*)

SOCIAL SCIENCES

Civics   Have students list the privileges, formerly available only to Egyptian kings, that were claimed by provincial governors and extended to ordinary Egyptians during the First Intermediate Period. What was the effect of this shift in privileges?

READING AND LANGUAGE ARTS

Reading Nonfiction   Reinforce for students that the divisions between periods of Egyptian history are not rigid. Have students point out indications of this in the chapter, such as on page 67.

Using Language   Have students note the use of similes in the extracts ("the land turns around as does a potter's wheel," page 64; "the whole country has become like locusts," page 65).

SUPPORTING LEARNING

English Language Learners   Students can work in pairs to retell different parts of *The Tale of Sinuhe* in their own words.

Struggling Readers   Have students use the outline graphic organizer in the back of this guide to understand the characteristics of the First Intermediate Period and the Middle Kingdom as described in the chapter.

EXTENDING LEARNING

Enrichment   Students can learn more about the archaeological exploration of Kahun, a Middle Kingdom village mentioned in the chapter, and take a virtual tour of Kahun at *http://kahun.man.ac.uk/virtual_kahun1.htm*.

Extension   Have students work in groups to dramatize different scenes in *The Tale of Sinuhe*. Students can use details from the chapter or from the excerpts in *The World in Ancient Times Primary Sources and Reference Volume*.

WRITING

Narration
Distribute copies of the blackline master for Chapter 8. In retelling the Sinuhe story in a comic strip, have students demonstrate their understanding of the main points of the story and its moral.

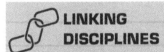

LINKING DISCIPLINES

Science Have students investigate the work of archaeobotanists to learn more about how ancient vegetation can lead to conclusions about the past, such as those described on page 68.

SINUHE'S STORY

Directions

Retell the story of Sinuhe as a comic strip by filling in the panel for each scene with a drawing of Sinuhe and text in speech balloons. Then answer the questions in complete sentences.

Sinuhe flees Egypt.	**Sinuhe is rescued by nomads.**
Sinuhe wants to return to Egypt.	**Sinuhe's happy ending.**

1. Why do you think King Senwosert welcomed Sinuhe back?

_____

_____

2. What is the moral of the story of Sinuhe?

_____

_____

NAME _____ **DATE** _____

A. MULTIPLE CHOICE

Circle the letter of the best answer for each question.

1. Which of the following was **not** a result of the governors of Egypt gaining power?
   a. The king lost power.
   b. Grain was kept in the provinces.
   c. Governors lived in the capital city.
   d. Civil wars broke out.

2. After King Pepi II died, Egypt entered a dark period because
   a. only the Greeks wrote about Egypt.
   b. no king had the power to pull the country together again.
   c. the country was invaded by outsiders.
   d. no new literature was being written.

3. With the decline of the king's power, Egyptians started to
   a. destroy the statues of the gods.
   b. experiment with new style and inventions.
   c. lose belief in their gods.
   d. learn how to read and write.

4. Which statement about the Middle Kingdom is true?
   a. Centralized power returned.
   b. The king lost power.
   c. Chaos was everywhere.
   d. Civil wars raged.

5. The moral of the *Tale of Sinuhe* was that Egypt was
   a. destined to become great.
   b. not a good place to live.
   c. the finest country in the world.
   d. better off when kings did not rule.

B. SHORT ANSWER

Write one or two sentences to answer each question.

6. Why was Egypt a land of feeble kingdoms during the First Intermediate Period?
   _____
   _____

7. What positive results came from the turmoil of the First Intermediate Period?
   _____
   _____

8. How does the *Tale of Sinuhe* describe a Middle Kingdom palace?
   _____
   _____

C. ESSAY

Using details from the chapter, write an essay on a separate sheet of paper contrasting the view that later writers had of the First Intermediate period with Egyptians' actual experience during that time.

TAKE TWO MICE AND CALL ME IN THE MORNING: MEDICINE AND MAGIC
PAGES 70–74

CAST OF CHARACTERS

Homer Greek poet; author of the *Iliad* and the *Odyssey*

Diodorus (die-uh-DOR-us) **Siculus** (SICK-u-lus) Greek historian who wrote 40 books of world history

THEN and NOW

Researchers excavating a tomb in the ancient city of Thebes found a wooden toe attached to a mummy's foot. The find was reported in a British medical journal as an example of the skill of ancient Egyptian doctors. The wooden toe showed signs of wear, indicating it had been in use while the person, a woman in her 50s, was alive. Invite students to write a story about the doctor who designed the wooden toe.

CHAPTER SUMMARY

In ancient times, medical care in Egypt was considered the best in the world. Doctors studied textbooks, trained in specialties, and were guided by laws. From indigestion and the common cold to asthma and brain surgery, their cures were world renowned.

PERFORMANCE OBJECTIVES

▶ To comprehend the depth of ancient Egyptians' understanding of injury and disease
▶ To describe ancient Egyptian medical training and health concerns
▶ To understand how ancient Egyptian treatments for certain illnesses were similar to and different from treatments today

BUILDING BACKGROUND

Ask students what they did to feel better the last time they had a cold. Remind them that there are ways to treat a cold's symptoms but as yet no cure for the common cold. Explain that in this chapter they will be learning how ancient Egyptian doctors treated illnesses.

WORKING WITH PRIMARY SOURCES

The chapter includes quotes from the Ebers Papyrus and the Edwin Smith Papyrus. Have students find out more about these important documents that reveal the world of Egyptian medicine. A portion of the Edwin Smith Papyrus is available in translation online at *www.neurosurgery.org/cybermuseum/pre20th/ epapyrus.html*.

GEOGRAPHY CONNECTION

Location Have students investigate the source of the obsidian that Egyptian surgeons used. Explain that obsidian is volcanic glass, so they will be looking for a place or places with volcanoes, close enough to trade with Egypt (possible sites: Italy, central Africa). When students have determined possible sources for the obsidian, have them locate the places on a map of the region. Have interested students find out more about the geological processes that make obsidian in the ground and give an oral report to the class.

READING COMPREHENSION QUESTIONS

1. Who could be found studying in houses of life (*peru-ankh*)? (*medical students*)
2. When would an ancient Egyptian doctor use a magic spell as a treatment? (*when a disease was caused by germs, which were too small to see*)
3. What do honey and onions have in common as remedies? (*They are antibiotics.*)
4. Distribute copies of the blackline master for Chapter 9. Have students in the role of ancient Egyptian doctors answer questions based on the chapter.

CRITICAL THINKING QUESTIONS

1. How did Egyptian doctors get their medical knowledge? (*by studying the writings of famous doctors who had come before; from experience with many patients*)

2. What would a patient's family have to prove for an Egyptian doctor to be convicted of malpractice? (*They would have to prove that the doctor had not followed the written rules for treating the illness.*)

3. Summarize evidence that Egyptian physicians were skilled at treating illnesses. (*They specialized; they trained, using written texts and records of past experience; they prescribed remedies based on the age and size of the patient; they used anesthesia during surgeries; and they knew what illnesses they could not treat.*)

SOCIAL SCIENCES

Science, Technology, and Society   Have students investigate the influence of Egyptian physicians, surgeons, and medical schools on other civilizations, as attested by Homer and other Greek writers mentioned in the chapter. Students can begin their research at *http://medweb.bham.ac.uk/histmed/pahor.html*. Have them report their findings orally to the class.

READING AND LANGUAGE ARTS

Reading Nonfiction   Have students locate places in the chapter where the authors compare and contrast Egyptian medical practices and remedies with those of doctors today. Have students make a chart showing the comparisons and contrasts.

Using Language   Have students investigate the origins of these words found in the chapter: *medicine, physician, prescription, anesthesia*. Have them discuss the results of their research in class.

SUPPORTING LEARNING

English Language Learners   Have partners list nouns they find in the chapter that relate to illness and cures, such as *indigestion, cold, asthma, antibiotic*. Partners should then define these words from the context and use them in a sentence.

Struggling Readers   Have students make a chart with details of the kinds of cures ancient Egyptian doctors used.

EXTENDING LEARNING

Enrichment   Have a group of students investigate present-day research into the antibiotic properties of honey and onions and then present their findings to the class.

Extension   Have students role-play the doctor's visit to a sick child described on page 74.

WRITING

Persuasion Have students use information from the chapter to write a letter from an ancient Egyptian to a friend in another country. The letter should recommend that the friend come to Egypt for treatment by an Egyptian doctor—"the best in the world."

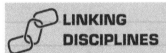
LINKING DISCIPLINES

Health Egyptian doctors prescribed garlic for many illnesses. Have students research information about the health benefits of garlic that are recognized today and summarize them in a short essay.

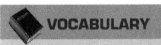
VOCABULARY

peru-ankh houses of life (libraries) where medical records and texts were kept

MEDICAL ADVICE Q & A

Directions

Read each question and then answer it as an ancient Egyptian doctor might have, based on information in Chapter 9. Use complete sentences.

1. What treatment do you recommend for asthma?

_____

_____

2. My baby has a cough. What can I do?

_____

_____

3. My daughter wants to be a doctor. What kind of training can she expect?

_____

_____

4. My relative died after being treated by a doctor. Should the doctor be punished? Why or why not?

_____

_____

5. Night after night my brother has terrible indigestion. What can we do?

_____

_____

6. Is it true that honey is a good treatment for an infection? What else could I use?

_____

_____

7. Is there any disease you won't treat?

_____

_____

8. What are the pros and cons of being a doctor in ancient Egypt?

_____

_____

NAME   **DATE**

A. MULTIPLE CHOICE

Circle the letter of the best answer for each question.

1. Ancient Egyptian doctors were able to recognize a disease by
   a. reading signs from the gods.
   b. making sacrifices.
   c. performing surgery on the patient.
   d. finding out the patient's symptoms.

2. The Ebers Papyrus shows that Egyptian doctors had
   a. many cures for injury and disease.
   b. to guess at which cure to use.
   c. serious gaps in their medical knowledge.
   d. few rules to follow in treating patients.

3. Egyptians thought that diseases caused by germs they couldn't see were the result of
   a. unhealthy diet.
   b. demons.
   c. bad water.
   d. insects.

4. The symptoms that led a doctor to say "death threatens" are recognized today as the symptoms of which disease?
   a. blood poisoning
   b. stomach cancer
   c. broken leg
   d. heart attack

5. Why might an ancient Egyptian doctor have prescribed garlic?
   a. to treat asthma
   b. to fight bacteria
   c. to help women give birth
   d. to use in an amulet

B. SHORT ANSWER

Write one or two sentences to answer each question.

6. Why do archaeologists believe that Egyptian surgeons used anesthesia?
   _____
   _____

7. What kinds of surgery did Egyptian doctors perform?
   _____
   _____

8. Why were honey and garlic effective in fighting disease?
   _____
   _____

C. ESSAY

Using details from the chapter, write an essay on a separate sheet of paper comparing and contrasting the techniques of ancient Egyptian doctors with the techniques doctors use today.

FOR HOMEWORK

**STUDENT
STUDY GUIDE**

pages 29–30

**CAST OF
CHARACTERS**

Manetho (MAN-eh-tho)
Egyptian priest and
historian; first to divide
Egypt's pharaohs into
dynasties

Seqenenre (seck-EN-
en-re) king of Egypt;
fought against the
Hyksos; killed in battle

Ahmose (AHK-moz)
Egyptian soldier who
fought against the Hyksos

Ahhotep (ah-HOE-tep) I
queen of Egypt; mother
of the Egyptian kings
who expelled the Hyksos
from Egypt

Josephus (jo-SEE-fus)
Flavius Jewish general
turned Roman historian

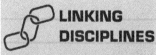
**LINKING
DISCIPLINES**

Art Have students trace
the chariot and driver in
the picture on page 79.
They can add color and
write text explaining the
importance of the
chariot to the Egyptians
of this period.

CHAPTER SUMMARY

In the Second Intermediate Period, the Hyksos invaded and occupied northern
Egypt. Though they adopted Egyptian ways and introduced foods and tools that
the Egyptians in turn adopted from them, the Hyksos were still considered
"foreign." Eventually, the Egyptian king, Seqenenre, gathered and trained an
effective army and drove out the Hyksos.

PERFORMANCE OBJECTIVES

▶ To summarize the Hyksos contributions to Egypt
▶ To understand how wars were fought in ancient Egypt
▶ To recognize the reasons for the Egyptians' victory over the Hyksos

BUILDING BACKGROUND

Discuss the exchange of foods among countries. Ask: What foods from the
United States are now found in other countries? What foods available here come
from other countries? Explain that in this chapter students will meet the Hyksos,
foreigners to ancient Egypt, who brought apples and olives to Egypt but who
were not welcome there.

WORKING WITH PRIMARY SOURCES

Have a group of students read more about the Hyksos in translations of Manetho
and Josephus Flavius online at *http://nefertiti.iwebland.com/manetho_hyksos.htm*.
Have them share the results of their research with the class.

GEOGRAPHY CONNECTION

Movement The Hyksos were invaders who came "from the east." Ask
students to research more about the Hyksos and to locate the limits of their
settlement in Egypt. Students can find information about the Hyksos at
www.touregypt.net/featurestories/hyksos.htm, recommended in the Websites section
of their book.

READING COMPREHENSION QUESTIONS

1. What did the Hyksos king use as an excuse to start a war with Egypt's King
   Seqenenre? (*The Hyksos king complained that Seqenenre's hippos "kept him
   awake at night with their grunts."*)
2. Which Hyksos technology did the Egyptian army improve on? How? Why?
   (*The Egyptians took the Hyksos chariot design. They made it lighter and covered
   the axle with metal to make it easier for a horse to pull. They put two men in the
   chariot—a driver and a soldier. These improvements made chariots more useful in
   battle, which gave the Egyptians an advantage over the Hyksos.*)
3. What was the Golden Fly and its connection to Ahmose? (*The Golden Fly was a
   medal of honor given only to the bravest soldiers. Ahmose received seven.*)
4. Distribute copies of the blackline master for Chapter 10. Have students use
   information in the chapter to compare the Hyksos and Egyptian armies.

CRITICAL THINKING QUESTIONS

1. What would you expect Egypt to be like during the Second Intermediate Period? (*a time without a strong king; possibly a time of warfare within Egypt*)
2. What did the Hyksos do that made the Egyptians angry? (*They took over an area of Egypt and set up their own kingdom. They fortified the city of Avaris and made it their capital. They seemed to be trying to steal Egyptian medical secrets. They insulted the king of Egypt.*)
3. Explain the chapter title "Hands Off." (*The title refers to the Egyptians' final victory over the Hyksos which resulted in their leaving Egypt. Their departure showed that the Egyptians were strong enough to say "Hands off" to invaders.*)

SOCIAL SCIENCES

Science, Technology, and Society   Have a group of students locate pictures of Egyptian chariots in books or online resources. Have the group create a display showing how Egyptians improved the chariot design they took from the Hyksos.

READING AND LANGUAGE ARTS

Reading Nonfiction   Few dates are used in this chapter, yet the writing indicates the passage of many years. Have students estimate the length of the Hyksos influence in Egypt from the descriptions in the text. (Historians now mostly agree that there were six Hyksos kings in Egypt, reigning for 108 years, although they did not control all of Egypt.)

Using Language   Point out the similes in the first sentence on page 75: "swoop across Egypt like a tidal wave," and in the first paragraph on page 77: "like a pebble in the Egyptian king's sandal." Define *simile,* and elicit the unlike subjects in these examples. Have students make up their own similes describing the Hyksos in Egypt.

SUPPORTING LEARNING

Struggling Readers   Have students use the cause and effect chart in the back of this guide to show the impact the superior Hyksos army had on the Egyptians. When students have completed their charts, have them evaluate whether the results were positive for the Egyptians.

EXTENDING LEARNING

Enrichment   Have small groups discover more about the Hyksos: where they might have come from, how long their migration into Egypt took, other aspects of their culture, and so on. Groups should report their findings to the class.

Extension   Have students design a modern medal for bravery, like the Egyptians' Golden Fly. As the horsefly was the "tormentor of beasts," students should have an explanation of why their medal represents bravery.

WRITING

Interview Have students work in pairs to create questions to ask an Egyptian soldier about the army on the eve of the Battle of Avaris. Students can exchange questions and write answers based on information in the chapter.

VOCABULARY

heqa-khasut "chiefs of foreign lands," the Egyptians' word for the invaders the Greeks called the Hyksos

THEN and NOW

At the site of a city known as Tharo in ancient times, three fortresses have been excavated. Each was built on the ruins of the one before, and together they underline the importance of Tharo. The earliest fortress dates back to the age of the Hyksos. Ask students to locate Tharo on a map of ancient Egypt to see why it was known as the eastern gateway to the Nile Valley.

NAME   DATE

COMPARING THE HYKSOS AND EGYPTIAN ARMIES

Directions

Complete the chart with information from the chapter. Then describe these points, using complete sentences.

	Hyksos Army	Egyptian Army	
		At first battles with Hyksos	At Battle of Avaris
Soldiers			
Weapons			
Training			
Chariots			
Armor			
Style of Fighting			

Write a paragraph describing the changes the Egyptians made in their army and why they made them.

_____

_____

_____

_____

_____

CHAPTER TEST 10
THE ANCIENT EGYPTIAN WORLD

A. MULTIPLE CHOICE

Circle the letter of the best answer for each question.

1. Which of the following is **not** something introduced to Egypt by the Hyksos?
   a. Zebu cattle
   b. olives
   c. pyramids
   d. war chariots

2. When the authors write, "What had once been a rag-tag scrabble of men became an organized military," which group are they describing?
   a. King Seqenenre's palace guard
   b. the Hyksos army
   c. the Egyptian army
   d. Queen Ahhotep's guards

3. In an early battle against the Hyksos, the Egyptian King Seqenenre died from which of the following causes?
   a. trampling by a hippo
   b. a disease brought by the Hyksos
   c. a wound to the heart
   d. a wound to the skull

4. In which part of Egypt did the Hyksos settle?
   a. northern Egypt
   b. southern Egypt
   c. Sahara Desert
   d. entire Nile Valley

5. Which adjective describes the Egyptian army that besieged the Hyksos at the last battle of Avaris?
   a. part-time
   b. lightly armored
   c. untrained
   d. well-trained

B. SHORT ANSWER

Write one or two sentences to answer each question.

6. How did the Egyptians improve upon the design of the Hyksos chariots?

   _____

   _____

7. What did the Egyptians have to improve besides their training in order to beat the Hyksos?

   _____

   _____

8. How did the conflict between the Hyksos and the Egyptians end?

   _____

   _____

C. ESSAY

The chapter says, "It didn't matter if they worshipped Egyptian gods, wore Egyptian clothes, or ate Egyptian food. They were still foreigners." Use the information in the chapter to write an essay on a separate sheet of paper explaining Egyptian hostility to the Hyksos.

CHAPTER 11

A TALE OF TWO DEITIES: HATSHEPSUT AND THUTMOSE III

PAGES 81–87

FOR HOMEWORK

STUDENT STUDY GUIDE

pages 31–32

CAST OF CHARACTERS

Hatshepsut (hat-SHEP-soot) female "king" of Egypt; ruled in place of her stepson Thutmose III for nearly 20 years

Thutmose (TUT-moze) **II** king of Egypt during Dynasty 18

Thutmose (TUT-moze) **III** king of Egypt; stepson of Queen Hatshepsut; fought against the Canaanites at the Battle of Megiddo, the first recorded battle in history

THEN and **NOW**

Egyptians usually painted portraits in profile, but Spanish researchers have discovered a frontal portrait of a pharaoh that represents either Hatshepsut or Thutmose III. Have students find out more about Egyptian art using the sources in the Further Reading list at the back of their book.

CHAPTER SUMMARY

In order to rule Egypt, Queen Hatshepsut had to claim to be a king and dress the part, complete with a false beard. Her achievements, which included a spectacular trading voyage to fabled Punt, and her very existence were all but erased after her death by Thutmose III, who secured Egypt's preeminence in trade by defeating rebels at the battle of Megiddo.

PERFORMANCE OBJECTIVES

▶ To describe the reign of Queen Hatshepsut (and why she had to be called a king)
▶ To summarize the story of Hatshepsut's trading expedition to Punt
▶ To understand King Thutmose III's tactics at the Battle of Megiddo

BUILDING BACKGROUND

Encourage students to share stories that bring families together. These may be stories of their family, or families they have read about. Explain that this chapter is based on favorite stories that two pharaohs told about themselves.

WORKING WITH PRIMARY SOURCES

Refer students to the *World in Ancient Times Primary Sources and Reference Volume,* which contains an excerpt from royal inscriptions about Hatshepsut's expedition to Punt. Have students read the excerpt aloud in small groups and then analyze how Hatshepshut tied the expedition to the approval of the god Amun.

GEOGRAPHY CONNECTION

Place Have students use the map and map scale on page 86 to calculate the distance between Thebes and Punt (via the Red Sea).

READING COMPREHENSION QUESTIONS

1. What do the inscriptions on Hatshepsut's tomb indicate about the location of Punt? (*African animals shown in the inscriptions show that Punt was farther south in Africa than Egypt.*)
2. What were some of the goods the expedition brought back from Punt? (*ebony, ivory, monkeys, fragrant woods, eye cosmetics*)
3. How did an Egyptian queen's power differ from a king's? (*A king was a god and acted as a middleman between the gods and the people; a queen had limited powers and needed to govern with a coruler.*)
4. How did Thutmose's daring bring victory at Megiddo? (*Thutmose led his army through a narrow, dangerous pass to the city of Megiddo. The defenders, not expecting him to take that route, had left it mostly undefended. The soldiers of Megiddo had to retreat to their walled city, which Thutmose then besieged for months until it surrendered.*)

CRITICAL THINKING QUESTIONS

1. Why do you think Hatshepsut wanted people to remember the expedition to Punt? (*It showed how her leadership added to Egypt's wealth and made the country flourish. It promoted the idea that a queen could bring* ma'at *and so could be a fit ruler of Egypt.*)

2. Why do you suppose the time of Thutmose III's reign would be a golden age, as the authors say at the end of the chapter? (*Possible answer: The Egyptian army was powerful enough to control lands outside of Egypt. Trade and exploration had begun to expand under Hatshepsut and would most likely continue under Thutmose. New materials and new contacts would probably bring different ideas in the arts to Egypt.*)

3. Distribute copies of the blackline master for Chapter 11 and have students review the accomplishments of Hatshepsut and Thutmose III.

SOCIAL SCIENCES

Civics Have students summarize the reasons why Queen Hatshepsut needed to be a king in order to rule Egypt and the steps she took to become one.

READING AND LANGUAGE ARTS

Reading Nonfiction Read aloud the title and first paragraph of the chapter. Ask: How effective is this as an opening device? As students read, ask them to note further references to stories and storytelling. After students finish reading, discuss their assessment of the technique of framing the chapter with a discussion of storytelling.

Using Language Remind students that in English, proper nouns, such as the names of people, time periods, countries, wars, battles, rivers, and places are capitalized. Assign small groups a section of the chapter and have them list the proper nouns they find to sort into categories.

SUPPORTING LEARNING

English Language Learners Encourage students to work in small groups to write down favorite family stories from their own experience or ones they have read about and then read them aloud.

Struggling Readers Have students use the main idea map graphic organizer at the back of this guide to analyze Queen Hatshepsut's expedition to Punt. They might write *Expedition* in the central circle, and the headings *Travel to Punt, Gifts from Hatshepsut, Products of Punt,* and *Results of the Trip* in the surrounding circles. Students should then add details from the chapter for each category.

EXTENDING LEARNING

Enrichment Students can view a map and read more about the Battle of Megiddo online *at http://nefertiti.iwebland.com/megiddobattle.htm,* recommended in the Websites section in their book.

Extension Invite students to draw an annotated diagram showing King Thutmose III's choice of routes as he led his army to Megiddo.

WRITING

Dialogue Ask students to work in small groups to write a dialogue between Thutmose III and one of his advisers at the war council based on information from page 87. In the dialogue, Thutmose III should explain why he has chosen to lead his army on the most direct route to attack Megiddo. The adviser should raise questions about these decisions. Students can act out their dialogues for the class.

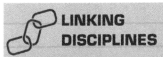
LINKING DISCIPLINES

Art Have students examine the carving from Hatshepsut's temple on page 83. Students can make their own drawings of the carving and discuss why she chose to be shown as a man.

COMPARING RULERS

Directions

Complete the chart with information from the chapter about Hatshepsut and Thutmose III.

	Hatshepsut	Thutmose III
Leadership		
Relations with Other Countries		
Contributions to Egypt		

NAME **DATE**

A. MULTIPLE CHOICE

Circle the letter of the best answer to each question.

1. How did Queen Hatshepshut become king of Egypt?
   a. She poisoned the previous ruler.
   b. Her husband died and her son was too young to rule by himself.
   c. Her father died and had no other children.
   d. Her father overthrew the previous ruler, but died in the battle.

2. How did Hatshepsut convince Egyptians that she was the child of the god Amun?
   a. She built a temple to the god.
   b. She forced them to believe or be thrown in jail.
   c. She made up a story about her birth and had artists illustrate it.
   d. She started a new religion with herself at the head.

3. Hatshepsut's expedition to Punt shows that she added to Egypt's wealth through
   a. conquest.
   b. trade and exploration.
   c. buying territory.
   d. naval victories.

4. King Thutmose III was a skilled warrior because he
   a. read histories about Egyptian wars.
   b. followed the ideas of generals.
   c. spent his childhood in a foreign country.
   d. trained with the army when he was young.

5. Thutmose III succeeded at Megiddo because he
   a. showed bold leadership in surprising the enemy.
   b. had a fleet of ships that could navigate the Red Sea.
   c. had help from Hatshepsut.
   d. led the army on the easiest route to meet the enemy.

B. SHORT ANSWER

Write one or two sentences to answer each question.

6. What riches did Hatshepshut's trade expedition bring back from Punt?

   _____

   _____

7. Why was it necessary for Thutmose III to attack Megiddo?

   _____

   _____

8. What decision did Thutmose III make that helped the Egyptians beat the rebel army at Megiddo?

   _____

   _____

C. ESSAY

Choose either Hatshepsut or Thutmose III and write an essay on a separate sheet of paper answering this question: What was the pharaoh's contribution to Egypt? Include information from the chapter about the pharaoh's abilities and accomplishments.

THE NEW KINGDOM

PAGES 88–114

UNIT OBJECTIVES

Unit 4 focuses on rulers who reigned during the years 1386–1325 BCE, ancient Egypt's golden age. Students will encounter one of the most recognizable of ancient Egyptians—Nefertiti, wife of Akhenaten. In this unit your students will learn

▶ about ancient Egyptians' lifestyles and their obsession with appearances.
▶ how pharaohs governed and conducted diplomacy.
▶ about the upheaval in Egyptian life caused by Akhenaten's religious fervor.

PRIMARY SOURCES

Unit 4 includes pictures of artifacts/excerpts from the following primary sources:

▶ New Kingdom love poem
▶ Ebers Papyrus
▶ Last will and testament of Naunakhte
▶ *Tale of a Shipwrecked Sailor*
▶ *The Story of the Eloquent Peasant*
▶ New Kingdom love song lyrics
▶ Herodotus, *The Histories*
▶ Commemorative scarabs
▶ Tomb inscription from vizier of First Intermediate Period
▶ Text from tomb of Amenemhet, scribe
▶ Diodorus Siculus, *Histories*
▶ Amarna Letters
▶ Tablet from Tunip
▶ Proverb used by students
▶ Homer, the *Iliad*
▶ *The Great Hymn to the Aten*

BIG IDEAS IN UNIT 4

The big ideas in Unit 4 are **power, communication,** and **religion.** The pharaoh's power over his subjects, the vizier's powers as second in command to the pharaoh, and Egypt's power in the world are explored, as are the power of religious belief and the limited power of a ruler to change those beliefs. Such artifacts as the Amarna Letters and Amenhotep III's scarabs are examples of written communication used in wielding and maintaining power. Egyptians also communicated information about themselves and their social standing through makeup, clothing, wigs, and jewelry. Jewelry was particularly expressive, because Egyptians believed it had supernatural powers. Religious innovation during the Amarna Period under Amenhotep IV involved some wrenching changes affecting all Egyptians. As the newly named Akhenaten, the pharaoh instituted the worship of one god, the sun god Aten; cut off funds to temples and priests; and denied Egyptians the possibility of an afterlife. But even a pharaoh's absolute power could not change the religious beliefs of thousands of years.

GEOGRAPHY CONNECTION

During this period Amenhotep IV (Akhenaten) built a new capital, which is now called Amarna. Have students study the map of ancient Egypt on pages 12–13. Ask them to locate Amarna, Memphis, and Thebes and calculate the distances between them. Divide the class into small groups to investigate in more detail the natural features that made Amarna an appealing site for a new capital city.

TIMELINE

| 1386–1349 BCE | Reign of Amenhotep III, beginning of Egypt's golden age |
| 1350–1334 BCE | Reign of Akhenaten and Nefertiti; religious upheaval |

UNIT PROJECTS

Illustration

Invite students to illustrate one or more scenes from *The Tale of a Shipwrecked Sailor* (blackline master for Chapter 12). They might choose to show the serpent and sailor at their first encounter, the gifts the serpent gives the sailor, or the sailor waving to the ship that rescues him. Alternatively, students can retell the story as a comic book, providing illustrations and speech balloons.

Egyptian Beauty

Invite interested students to prepare an illustrated presentation about Egyptian ideals of beauty, using images from print and online resources. The presentation can include beauty products, jewelry, wigs, and images of beautiful women such as Nefertiti. Students can present their findings orally to the class.

Amarna Travel Guide

Have a group of students prepare and display a guidebook for travelers visiting Amarna in the time of Akhenaten and Nefertiti. The booklet can provide a brief history of the city, describe the new temple, and point out other notable buildings and the best spot to see the pharaoh and his wife and children.

Compare Reigns

Invite a panel of student "experts" to present a comparison of the reigns of Amenhotep III and his son, Akhenaten. The experts should investigate print and Internet resources to create a four-point comparison: domestic policy, foreign policy, religious observance, and overall impact of the reign.

ADDITIONAL ASSESSMENT

For Unit 4, divide the class into groups to work on the Compare Reigns project so you can assess their understanding the relationship between religion and the social and political order in Egypt as well as how Egypt was governed. Use the scoring rubric at the back of this guide to assess students' work, and have students rate their own work with the self-assessment rubric.

LITERATURE CONNECTION

A full translation of *The Great Hymn to Aten* is included in Simpson, *The Literature of Ancient Egypt*. Some resources are also available on-line, including *http://alexm.here.ru/mirrors/www.enteract.com/jwalz/Eliade/020.html*, which also provides text from *The Great Hymn to Aten*. For a classroom discussion, have students read portions of the hymn aloud and talk about what they think the excerpts mean. What words and phrases indicate this writing is a song of praise to a deity?

Suggest the following to students who want to read fiction about the period. (You might want to advise students that historical fiction is not always accurate in its details.)

► McCaughrean, Geraldine. *Casting the Gods Adrift: A Tale of Ancient Egypt.* Cricket Books, 2003. This fictional tale is based on Akhenhaten's (Amenhotep IV's) decree that all Egyptians worship a single god, Aten (the Sun God).

► Ross, Stewart. *Tales of the Dead: Ancient Egypt.* Dorling Kindersley Publishing, American Edition, 2003. This adventure story takes readers along with an embalmer when he raids a tomb in one of the pyramids around the time of Amenhotep III's reign.

UNIVERSAL ACCESS

The following strategies are designed to cover a range of learning styles and reading, language, and skill levels.

Reading Strategies

► To facilitate involvement with each chapter, have students learn more about the individuals mentioned by reading the Cast of Characters section of the book and doing small-group research into individual people.

► Call on students to read aloud sections of *The Tale of a Shipwrecked Sailor* (blackline master for Chapter 12). Encourage students to make their voices expressive and to use hand gestures where appropriate. Fit the passage to the reading abilities of each student.

Writing Strategies

► Have partners make a three-column chart with headings for each of the unit's big ideas. Partners should get together after reading each chapter to jot down their observations in each category.

► Have students create a cause and effect chart based on what happened in Egypt during the Amarna Period. The chart should connect Akhenaten's building of a new capital and attempts to change Egyptian religious beliefs with subsequent events in the Egyptian empire.

Listening and Speaking Strategies

▶ Have volunteers read aloud Chapter 12, assigning students different sections of the "fashion magazine"—clothing, jewelry, perfume, cosmetics, hair, and advice.

▶ Encourage a group of students to prepare and present a "Person in the Street" interview involving a reporter for an Egyptian newspaper and some Egyptians during the Amarna Period. The question could be, "What do you think about the new religion?" Responders can be for or against it and should present details from the book in support of their position.

UNIT VOCABULARY LIST

The following words that appear in Unit 4 are important for your students' understanding of the social studies content as well as for development of literacy. Use these words for vocabulary study or to reinforce language arts skills (e.g., synonyms, compound words, prefixes and suffixes, and related words). The words are listed below in the order in which they appear in the chapters.

Chapter 12	Chapter 13	Chapter 14	Chapter 15
grooming	essence	rubble	lion's share
profile	commemorate	antiquities	ambassador
conscious	scarab	curator	gratitude
accessory	commissioned	hoax	archives
supernatural	regal	seize	deformed
cosmetic	vizier	reputable	abscessed
straightforward	deed	dispatches	revenues
destination	ambitious	priceless	differentiated
pedicure	turmoil	correspondence	
alabaster	idyllic	grievance	
ceremony	elite	diplomacy	
meteoric	testimony	groveling	
lyrics	flogging	vassal	
ascertained	perjury	negotiations	

IN STYLE ALONG THE NILE: DAILY LIFE

PAGES 88–94

FOR HOMEWORK

STUDENT STUDY GUIDE

pages 33–34

THEN and NOW

Kohl eye makeup, like that used in ancient Egypt, is available today. Students can read more about kohl at *http://egyptmonth. com/mag09012000/ mag4.htm.*

 WRITING

○ **Personal Writing**
Have students create a diary entry written by an ancient Egyptian describing a party
○ he or she attended. They should include details about the guests' clothing, jewelry, hairstyles, music, and other
○ information from the chapter.

CHAPTER SUMMARY

In this chapter students learn about Egyptian views of beauty and style and the ways in which they communicated social status through fashion. The chapter is organized around topics found in fashion magazines today, including fashion and personal advice, book and music reviews, and a horoscope.

PERFORMANCE OBJECTIVES

► To describe some aspects of Egyptians' obsession with appearance
► To recognize the importance to Egyptians of the mischievous god Bes
► To delineate some similarities between ancient Egyptians and ourselves

BUILDING BACKGROUND

Ask students to describe some of today's fashion "dos and don'ts." Explain that in this chapter they will read about ancient Egyptian fashion, including makeup, jewelry, and the dos and don'ts of that day, such as wearing shoes outdoors (a don't) and shaving your head (a do—for both men and women).

WORKING WITH PRIMARY SOURCES

Students can find more about the last will and testament of Lady Naunakhte and related documents, as well as annotations explaining the meaning of the terms used in the documents, at *http://nefertiti.iwebland.com/texts/will_of_naunakhte.htm.* Have small groups read the documents and draw conclusions about the power Egyptian women had over their property.

GEOGRAPHY CONNECTION

Movement   Have students investigate ancient Egyptian trade and trade routes, and specifically the goods mentioned in the chapter, such as exports of perfumes and imports of silver.

READING COMPREHENSION QUESTIONS

1. What is some of the evidence that has led historians to conclude that ancient Egyptians cared about good grooming? (*the writings of Herodotus; drawings on tomb walls; the number and quality of cosmetic containers found in tombs*)
2. Why did it make sense for ancient Egyptians to shave their heads? (*Without hair it was easier to control the fleas and head lice that plagued ancient Egyptians.*)
3. Why did the book reviewer give a thumbs-down to *The Story of the Eloquent Peasant*? (*The complaining peasant was boring.*)
4. What was the point of wearing a wax cone on your head during a party in ancient Egypt? (*The scented wax cone melted during the party and perfumed the air.*)
5. Distribute copies of the blackline master for Chapter 12. Read aloud *The Tale of a Shipwrecked Sailor* and discuss students' answers to the questions.

CRITICAL THINKING QUESTIONS

1. What made the god Bes so popular? (*Bes, the god of the family, was very mischievous and amusing.*)

2. "You own your own property," says the advice columnist (the god Bes). To whom did Bes direct this statement, and why is that an unusual statement to make in ancient times? (*Bes makes this statement in answering a question from a "free woman." Unlike women in other parts of the ancient world, free Egyptian woman had rights; owning property was one of those rights.*)

3. Draw conclusions as to why Egyptian clothing stayed the same for thousands of years. (*Possible answer: Given the climate and other conditions, this was the most practical clothing for people to wear.*)

SOCIAL SCIENCES

Economics   Invite a group of students to investigate the economics of the teen beauty industry today and present their findings to the class. They can start their presentation by asking the rest of the class to estimate what they spend on hair and skin care products in the course of a year.

READING AND LANGUAGE ARTS

Reading Nonfiction   This chapter is divided into sections compatible with a fashion magazine of today. Have students identify the different sections (clothes, grooming, book reviews, horoscope, etc.) and evaluate the effectiveness of the chapter organization.

Using Language   Have students use a dictionary to discover the various meanings and etymology of the word *style* (from the Latin *stilus*, a writing instrument). Have students identify the definition closest to the way the word is used in this chapter (*the fashion of the moment, in style*). Then ask them to list and define other forms of the word (such as *stylish, stylist, stylistic*) and then use the words in a sentence.

SUPPORTING LEARNING

Struggling Readers   Have students use the outline graphic organizer in the back of this guide to analyze the topics covered in the chapter. They might include the following subjects: Clothes, Grooming, Fashion Dos and Don'ts, Advice, Book Reviews, and Horoscope, and then add details from the chapter under each one.

EXTENDING LEARNING

Enrichment   Interested groups of students can find out more about ancient Egyptian fashion and styles of dress in print resources and online at *www.touregypt. net/magazine/mag01012001/magf4.htm*. Tour Egypt is recommended in the Websites section of the student book. Students can download images and text and create an oral presentation for the class.

Extension   Invite students to draw a design for a "protective" piece of jewelry. (They can refer to the first paragraph on page 89 to review the description of ancient Egyptian protective designs.)

LINKING DISCIPLINES

Arithmetic Have students refer to the blackline master for Chapter 12 and note that the length of the shipwrecked sailor's ship and the size of the serpent are given in cubits. Have students translate cubits to feet and calculate the lengths, assuming one cubit equals 20.62 inches.

Directions

Read the story and then answer these questions on a separate sheet of paper, using complete sentences.

The Tale of a Shipwrecked Sailor

The sailor, back home in Egypt, starts his story:

Now I shall tell what happened to me. I was going to the mines of Pharaoh, and I went down on the sea in a ship of 150 cubits long and 40 cubits wide, with 150 sailors . . . whose hearts were stronger than lions. . . . [A]s we approached the land, the wind arose, and threw up waves eight cubits high. . . . [T]hose who were in the vessel perished, without one remaining. A wave threw me on an island. . . . I found there figs and grain, melons of all kinds, fishes, and birds.

Suddenly I heard a noise as of thunder, which I thought to be that of a wave of the sea. The trees shook, and the earth was moved. I uncovered my face, and I saw that a serpent drew near. He was 30 cubits long, and his beard greater than two cubits; his body was as overlaid with gold, and his color as that of true lazuli [blue]. . . . Then he . . . said, "What has brought you . . . to this isle?"

The sailor explained to the serpent how he came to be shipwrecked.

Then the serpent said to me . . . "You shall pass . . . four months in this isle. Then a ship shall come from your land with sailors, and you shall leave with them and go to your country."

In gratitude, the sailor told the serpent he would return to thank the serpent with sacred oils, perfumes, and incense as well as sacrificed birds and animals.

Then he smiled at my speech . . . [and] said to me: . . . "You are not rich in perfumes. . . . As for me, I am prince of the land of Punt, and I have perfumes. . . . [W]hen you depart from this place, you shall never see this isle again; it shall be changed into waves."

In time the ship appeared, as the serpent said it would. The serpent said farewell and wished the sailor well.

Then I bowed myself before him, and . . . he gave me gifts of precious perfumes, of cassia, of sweet woods, of kohl, of cypress, an abundance of incense, of ivory tusks, of baboons, of apes, and all kinds of precious things. . . . After this I went down to the shore . . . and I called to the sailors who were there.

1. What does the story tell you about what Egyptians prized and how they showed gratitude?

2. What does the serpent mean when he says the isle "shall be changed into waves"?

3. Identify references in the story to the following aspects of Egyptian life: mining, travel by sea, the power of serpents, the mysteries of Punt, pride in Egypt, loyalty to a ruler.

NAME   **DATE**

A. MULTIPLE CHOICE

Circle the letter of the best answer to each question.

1. Which of the following was **not** a concern of people in ancient Egypt?
   a. controlling body odor   **c.** keeping up with clothing styles
   b. curing baldness   **d.** using cosmetics

2. In ancient Egypt what was the difference between the clothing of a peasant and a rich person?
   a. the style of the clothes   **c.** the color of the clothes
   b. the fabric used to make clothes   **d.** the length of the clothes

3. Which statement describes ancient Egyptians' feelings about how they looked?
   a. They only cared about looking good in the afterlife.
   b. They wanted to look like Bes, the god of the family.
   c. They were obsessed with how they looked.
   d. They paid very little attention to how they looked.

4. Perfumes were popular in ancient Egypt. Which of the following groups made perfume and exported it?
   a. scribes   **c.** farmers
   b. royal servants   **d.** priests

5. Besides being fashionable, why did Egyptians wear gold and silver jewelry?
   a. to show off their wealth   **c.** because it had supernatural powers
   b. to show they were royalty   **d.** to make others jealous

B. SHORT ANSWER

Write one or two sentences to answer each question.

6. What dangers did the Egyptians believe jewelry guarded against?

_____

_____

7. Why did the Egyptians wear wigs rather than their natural hair?

_____

_____

8. Why didn't Egyptians wear clothing made from animal hides or hair?

_____

_____

C. ESSAY

**Using details from the fictional Egyptian fashion magazine in the chapter, write an essay on a
separate sheet of paper describing what a fashionable ancient Egyptian might have looked like.**

FOR HOMEWORK

**STUDENT
STUDY GUIDE**

pages 35–36

**CAST OF
CHARACTERS**

Amenhotep (ah-men-
HOE-tep) **III** king of Egypt
during Dynasty 18; in
contact with many
foreign countries

Tiy (tee) Egyptian queen;
married to Amenhotep
III; mother of Amenhotep
IV (Akhenaten)

THEN and **NOW**

Amenhotep III's claim to
fame today is that visitors
can see his home, the
largest remaining ancient
Egyptian royal palace.
Students can see a
picture of this royal
residence at *www.
touregypt.net/amentmpl.
htm*, recommended in
the "Websites" section of
their book.

CHAPTER SUMMARY

This chapter expands students' understanding of the pharaoh's power and the
extent of his control (through his vizier) over the lives of ordinary Egyptians.
The chapter also presents a grim reality of life for ordinary people and in
particular the harsh penalties imposed on them for breaking the law.

PERFORMANCE OBJECTIVES

▶ To summarize the duties of a pharaoh's vizier
▶ To describe some of the penalties for breaking the law in ancient Egypt
▶ To understand how Amenhotep communicated his accomplishments

BUILDING BACKGROUND

Ancient Egyptian rulers often gave themselves several complimentary names.
Explain that Amenhotep III named himself "The Dazzling Sun Disk." Have
students work with a partner and come up with two similar complimentary
names for each other.

WORKING WITH PRIMARY SOURCES

Have students locate the text of the scarab commemorating the marriage of
Amenhotep III and Tiy at *http://203.30.234.169/wam/exhibitions/online/egypt/
html/kingitem4.html*. Have them interpret what the multiple names of Amenhotep
refer to.

GEOGRAPHY CONNECTION

Location   Help students locate Medinet Habu (alternate names Djamet,
Tjamet) on a map or globe at 25° 43′ N, 32° 36′ E. Explain that latitude and
longitude coordinates make it possible to pinpoint any spot on earth. Medinet
Habu is the location of Amenhotep III's Malkata palace and the probable site of
the lake he had built for Queen Tiy. The town was located across the Nile River
from Thebes.

READING COMPREHENSION QUESTIONS

1. Why is *diplomacy* a good word to use in summing up Amenhotep III's reign?
   (*He kept in communication with other countries by sending scarabs about his
   achievements.*)
2. How did Amenhotep III show his devotion to his wife, Queen Tiy? (*He had a
   lake built for her, one mile long and a quarter of a mile wide.*)
3. Who are the three entities served by a vizier? (*the king, the gods, and the
   people*)
4. What group of Egyptian authorities reported to the vizier? (*governors*)
5. Distribute copies of the blackline master for Chapter 13 and have students
   complete the chart to organize information in the chapter about the role of
   vizier.

CRITICAL THINKING QUESTIONS

1. What might have been a problem for a weak pharaoh with a strong vizier? (*The vizier's powers might have led him to undermine the pharaoh.*)
2. Does the U.S. president have a vizier? (*Students should understand that the vizier's duties covered many areas that today are controlled by several different people.*)
3. Why was the crime of stealing punished severely in ancient Egypt? (*because everything in Egypt belonged to the king*)
4. Why is ancient Egyptian justice considered the "dark side" of ancient Egyptian life? (*because it was not justice as we know it; instead, it was arbitrary and cruel*)

SOCIAL SCIENCES

Civics   Have students make a chart comparing American justice with ancient Egyptian justice. For example, students might list the following statements about justice in the U.S. and counter each with a statement about ancient Egyptian justice: In the U.S., people are innocent until proven guilty, can confront witnesses, have a right to a jury of their peers, and cannot be subjected to cruel or unusual punishment.

READING AND LANGUAGE ARTS

Reading Nonfiction   Have students identify and assess the usefulness of the illustrations in this chapter. Have them suggest illustrations they would add to deepen understanding of the chapter.

Using Language   Have students add the following suffixes to the word *vizier: -ate* (office or authority of), *-ship* (status or rank of), *-ial* (of or pertaining to). Have students use these vizier-related words in sentences and then define *kingship, electorate,* and *managerial.*

SUPPORTING LEARNING

Struggling Readers   Have students use the main idea map graphic organizer in the back of this guide to analyze ancient Egyptian ideas about crime and punishment. They might write *crime and punishment* in the central circle and the headings *investigating crime, punishments,* and *prisons* in the surrounding circles. Students should then add details from the chapter for each category.

EXTENDING LEARNING

Enrichment   Have a group of students investigate ancient Egyptian news scarabs and then draw larger-than-life-size models to present to the class.

Extension   Ask students to create and act out skits based on scenes in the text. Student narrators can set the scene and describe the action.

WRITING

- **Explanation** Ask students to write a short essay agreeing or disagreeing with the statement "as long as government investigators had the power to torture suspects and witnesses, there could be no justice in ancient Egypt." Instruct them to include supporting details from the chapter.

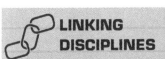

LINKING DISCIPLINES

Arithmetic Ask a small group of students to explain why a calendar based on a 365-day year with no leap year (the calendar used in ancient Egypt) results in total confusion about dates over the centuries.

NAME _____ **DATE** _____

DIAGRAMMING THE VIZIER'S DUTIES

Directions

Use the main idea map from the graphic organizers in the back of this book to explain the vizier's duties in each of the three major areas of his job. Add details to each of the outer circles. Then, on the lines below, write a short paragraph answering the question at the bottom of this page.

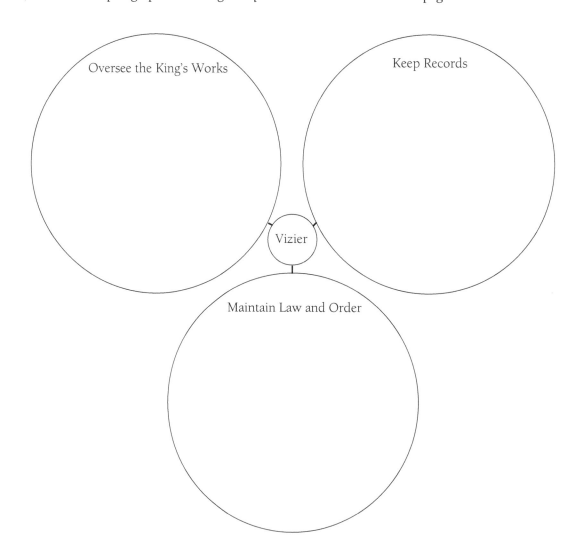

Why was the title "Eyes and Ears of the Sovereign" a good description of a vizier?

_____

_____

_____

_____

_____

NAME   **DATE**

A. MULTIPLE CHOICE

Circle the letter of the best answer to each question.

1. Amenhotep III sent bulletins about his kingdom to other countries using messages
   - **a.** memorized by couriers.
   - **b.** written on papyrus.
   - **c.** carved on scarabs.
   - **d.** on tomb walls.

2. Egyptians believed that if their king was successful at hunting, he would be successful
   - **a.** in trade.
   - **b.** on the battlefield.
   - **c.** in diplomacy.
   - **d.** in talking to the gods.

3. The job of the vizier was to
   - **a.** handle all of the tasks of running the country.
   - **b.** supervise the work of the many government officials.
   - **c.** send out news of the king's accomplishments.
   - **d.** be high priest of Amun.

4. Which of these was **not** a common punishment for a crime in ancient Egypt?
   - **a.** assignment to labor gang
   - **b.** cutting off the nose and ears
   - **c.** imprisonment
   - **d.** flogging

5. From our modern point of view, ancient Egyptian justice was very
   - **a.** advanced.
   - **b.** brutal.
   - **c.** inconsistent.
   - **d.** slow.

B. SHORT ANSWER

Write one or two sentences to answer each question.

6. Why were there probably not very many prisons in ancient Egypt?

_____

_____

7. Why did punishments for robbery become more severe in Amenhotep's time?

_____

_____

8. Who could become a vizier in Amenhotep's time?

_____

_____

C. ESSAY

The chapter states that the vizier "wore many hats." Write an essay on a separate sheet of paper explaining this statement. Include details about the vizier's job that support this statement.

THEN and NOW

A museum in Berlin, Germany (the Vorderasiatisches Museum, or VAM), houses 200 of the original Amarna Letters. All these letters have been photographed and are available online. This makes it possible for researchers to study the fragile tablets without handling them. Invite interested students to write a letter of appreciation to the museum.

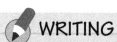 WRITING

- **News Article** Ask students to write a headline and a two-paragraph news article about the discovery of the Amarna Letters in 1887. Remind them to answer the questions *Who? What? Where? When? Why? How?*

CHAPTER SUMMARY

The chapter opens in the 19th century with a description of an English museum curator's efforts to obtain and interpret clay tablets whose value and content were at first unknown. Later the Amarna Letters, as the tablets came to be known, were found to contain priceless diplomatic correspondence from the reign of Amenhotep III.

PERFORMANCE OBJECTIVES

- ▶ To understand how diplomacy was carried out by Amenhotep III
- ▶ To recognize the extent of the Egyptian empire under Amenhotep III
- ▶ To explain the significance of the Amarna Letters and the efforts to gain control of them

BUILDING BACKGROUND

Ask: Do you or does anyone in your family save letters, post cards, souvenirs, or photographs? Do some family members call it "junk" and want to throw it away? Collect student responses and then tell them they will be reading about some really old letters that were saved, almost lost forever, and then saved again.

WORKING WITH PRIMARY SOURCES

Have students read more text from the Amarna Letters at *www.touregypt.net/featurestories/letters.htm,* recommended in the Websites section of their book.

GEOGRAPHY CONNECTION

Movement   The Amarna Letters are examples of the movement of information in the ancient world. Distribute copies of the blackline master for Chapter 14. Have students answer the questions using the map and map scale as well as information in the chapter.

READING COMPREHENSION QUESTIONS

1. Why was E. A. Wallis Budge interested in the clay tablets found at Amarna? (*He believed they might be ancient. If so, he wanted to buy them for the British Museum.*)
2. Who wrote the letters? (*The letters were from foreign rulers to Amenhotep III, his wife Tiy, and his son. Some were from independent foreign rulers, equal to the king of Egypt. Others were from vassals.*)
3. Some of the letters were complaints. What were the other letters about? (*demands for more gold, for more soldiers, for an Egyptian princess*)
4. How much time do the Amarna Letters cover? (*30 years*)

CRITICAL THINKING QUESTIONS

1. Why would the king of Babylon request a bride from Egypt? (*Having an Egyptian princess as a bride would have solidified the relationship between the king of Babylon and the king of Egypt, giving the Babylonian's demands higher priority in Egypt.*)
2. Why might Amenhotep III's son have ignored the pleas of foreign rulers? (*Possible answers: He may have been more interested in Egyptian matters. He may have been unable to help.*)
3. What evidence is there in the Amarna Letters that Amenhotep III had the upper hand over the King of Babylon? (*Amenhotep III refused the King of Babylon's request to marry an Egyptian princess.*)

SOCIAL SCIENCES

Civics   Invite students to discuss the ways in which diplomats and heads of state correspond with each other today. Examine the reasons why maintaining a written record of correspondence is important. Point out that phone calls between leaders and diplomats are logged, recorded, and transcribed to preserve a record.

READING AND LANGUAGE ARTS

Reading Nonfiction   Elicit that scholars have categorized the Amarna Letters into two main groups: those from rulers equal to the king of Egypt, and those from his vassals. Ask how else they might have categorized the letters. (*by country of origin, by ruler, by purpose*)

Using Language   Have students identify the simile in the first paragraph of the chapter (*"looked more like dog biscuits"*). Have them make up other similes about objects described in the chapter.

SUPPORTING LEARNING

English Language Learners   Have partners read sections of the chapter aloud to each other, define unfamiliar words, and then use the words in sentences.

Struggling Readers   Read aloud pages 101–103 (the story that frames the chapter), and then ask students to create a K-W-L chart like the sample in the back of this guide before reading the rest of the chapter.

EXTENDING LEARNING

Enrichment   Students can read more of the text of the Amarna Letters and clay tablets at *www.touregypt.net/featurestories/letters.htm*. Have them print out sample letters and read them aloud in an expressive voice.

Extension   Ask students to act out scenes from the text. For example, one student can narrate while a group acts out Budge's discussion with the messenger in Luxor about the fate of Monsieur Grebaut.

LINKING DISCIPLINES

Science Students can find out about research at Tel Aviv University, where scientists are using microscopes to investigate clay tablets such as the Amarna Letters. The link to the Laboratory for Comparative Microarchaeology and Metal Conservation is *www.tau.ac.il/ humanities/archaeology/ institute/facilities/ compmicroarch_ metalcon_lab.html.*

NAME **DATE**

MAP: FOREIGN RELATIONS OF THE NEW KINGDOM

Directions

Study the map. Then use information on the map and in Chapter 14 to answer the questions below.

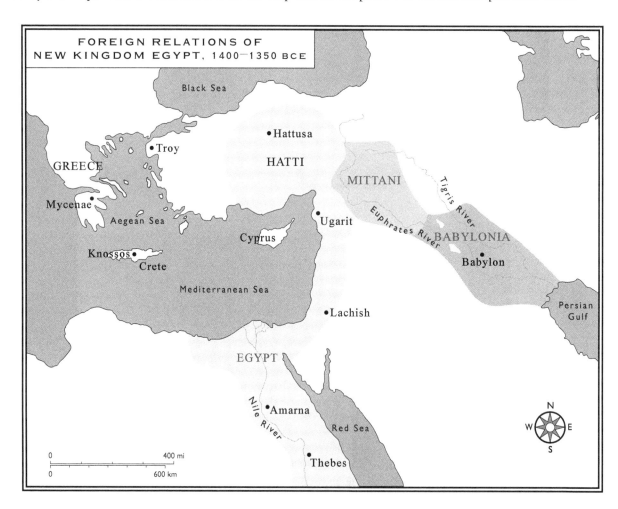

FOREIGN RELATIONS OF
NEW KINGDOM EGYPT, 1400—1350 BCE

1. Using the mileage scale, calculate the distance between Amarna and the following cities: Hattusa, Babylon, and Troy.

_____

2. Which city on the map is located farthest east? Which city is located farthest west?

_____

3. Which island city communicated with Egypt? How far is it by water from Amarna?

_____

4. What features do Mittani and Babylonia have in common?

_____

NAME _____ **DATE** _____

A. MULTIPLE CHOICE

Circle the letter of the best answer to each question.

1. Which of the following explains how the ancient Amarna Letters were first discovered in modern times?
   a. E. A. Wallis Budge found them at a shop in Luxor.
   b. A peasant woman found them in the ruins of Amarna.
   c. Monsieur Grebaut found them in Amarna.
   d. E. A. Wallis Budge found them on a train.

2. The Amarna Letters are communications between the king of Egypt and
   a. the vizier.
   b. foreign rulers.
   c. his wives.
   d. his children.

3. Based on the greetings of the letters, scholars group the letters as coming from
   a. African and Asian rulers.
   b. male and female rulers.
   c. independent rulers and vassals.
   d. Egyptian and Greek rulers.

4. The letters show that Amenhotep did not
   a. send gold to anyone.
   b. believe in diplomacy.
   c. keep good records.
   d. give away princesses.

5. The letters show that Amenhotep's son was
   a. attentive to foreign relations.
   b. was uninterested in diplomacy.
   c. a poor king.
   d. not married.

B. SHORT ANSWER

Write one or two sentences to answer each question.

6. What is a constant theme throughout the Amarna Letters?
   _____
   _____

7. What do the Amarna Letters tell us about the extent of Egyptian influence during Amenhotep's reign?
   _____
   _____

8. What do you suppose happened to the vassals of Egypt during the reign of Amenhotep's son?
   _____
   _____

C. ESSAY

Write an essay on a separate sheet of paper summarizing how a number of the Amarna Letters wound up in the possession of the British Museum. Include your conclusions about why such a process probably would not happen today.

**CAST OF
CHARACTERS**

Amenhotep (ah-men-HOE-tep) **IV** or **Akhenaten** (ahk-ken-NAH-ton) king of Egypt who replaced worship of the gods of Egypt with worship of a single god, Aten (the Sun disk)

Nefertiti (nef-er-TEE-tee) queen of Egypt; wife of Amenhotep IV/Akhenaten; known for her beauty; perhaps the power behind the throne

THEN and **NOW**

The Egyptian National Museum in Cairo wants the Egyptian Museum in Berlin, Germany, to return an ancient statue of Nefertiti to Egypt on the grounds that it was removed illegally from Egypt in 1913. Ask students to write a brief statement agreeing or disagreeing that ancient artifacts taken from their original country should be returned.

CHAPTER SUMMARY

When Amenhotep IV took the throne, he changed not only his name (to Akhenaten) but also Egypt's religion. Instead of many gods, Egyptians were told to worship only one: Aten, the sun god. The chapter describes Akhenaten's obsessive efforts to achieve this goal.

PERFORMANCE OBJECTIVES

▶ To understand Akhenaten's efforts to change Egyptian religion and the reasons why they failed
▶ To evaluate the place of Nefertiti in Egyptian history
▶ To describe the new capital city's location and major buildings

BUILDING BACKGROUND

Ask students how they think Americans would react to a proposal to move the U.S. capital from Washington, D.C., to another city. Explain that in this chapter they will meet an Egyptian pharaoh who not only moved the Egyptian capital but also imposed a new religion on the Egyptian people.

WORKING WITH PRIMARY SOURCES

Refer students to *The World in Ancient Times Primary Sources and Reference Volume* for a more complete version of *The Great Hymn to the Aten*. After students read the hymn, have them answer the question: According to Akhenaten, why is Aten worthy of praise?

GEOGRAPHY CONNECTION

Location   Have students locate Amarna on the map on page 108 and describe its location relative to Memphis and Thebes. Students can use the map scale to calculate the distance between Amarna and the other two cities.

READING COMPREHENSION QUESTIONS

1. Why was the time of Amenhotep's youth a golden age for Egypt? (*Egypt's empire was huge. Gold from Nubia swelled its treasury. Tribute payments flowed in from neighboring rulers. Huge buildings were constructed.*)
2. When during his reign did Amenhotep IV change his name to Akhenaten and why? (*in the fifth year of his reign; because he changed the religion at that time and wanted to show his allegiance with the new god*)
3. What steps did Akhenaten take to change the Egyptian religion? (*He declared that the old Egyptian gods no longer existed; that Aten was the one and only god. He cut off payments to other temples. He decreed that only he could represent Aten on Earth. He denied Egyptians the afterlife.*)
4. Distribute copies of the blackline master for Chapter 15 and have students answer the questions there about Akhenaten's capital city.

CRITICAL THINKING QUESTIONS

1. Judging by the evidence in the chapter, could Akhenaten have successfully established his new religion? (*As all-powerful ruler he might have been able to establish his own religion, but he made mistakes, including losing the support of the priests and denying the afterlife to Egyptians.*)

2. What long-term effects did Akhenaten's reign have on Egypt and its empire? (*Egypt was ignored while Akhenaten concentrated on his religion and his new city. Foreign subjects fell to outside conquerors. The empire went into decline.*)

SOCIAL SCIENCES

Science, Technology, and Society Have students investigate the layout and construction of the workers' village in Amarna and share their findings with the class. Instruct them to draw conclusions about these buildings: Why were they built the way they were? What were the benefits and drawbacks of their construction and layout? How does the village compare with villages today? Information can be found at *www.touregypt.net/featurestories/ easternvillage.htm,* recommended in the Websites section of the student book.

READING AND LANGUAGE ARTS

Reading Nonfiction Point out the sidebar One and Only on page 110, which introduces the idea that Akhenaten was a monotheist. Write *monotheist* and *polytheist* on the board. Elicit the meanings of *mono-* ("one") and *poly-* ("many").

Using Language Introduce foreshadowing by reading aloud the sentence from paragraph one on page 112: "The name change was not as shocking as what followed." Elicit that this sentence is a signal for readers to expect something very significant, in this case Akhenaten's announcement that the old gods no longer existed.

SUPPORTING LEARNING

Struggling Readers Have students use a two-column comparison chart to compare the religion imposed by Akhenaten to the traditional Egyptian religion. Under the headings *New* and *Traditional*, they can organize information in these categories: number of gods, forms of worship, beliefs about the afterlife.

EXTENDING LEARNING

Enrichment Encourage students to find out more about the life of Nefertiti, with particular emphasis on the part she played in Akhenaten's life and rule.

Extension Have students role-play a scene where two ancient Egyptians are discussing changes Amenhotep IV has decreed. One person can be resisting the changes and the other willing to go along to see what will happen.

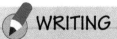
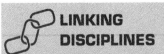

MAP OF AKHENATEN'S CAPITAL CITY

Directions

Study the diagram of the city of Amarna. Then use the information in the diagram and in Chapter 15 to answer the questions below.

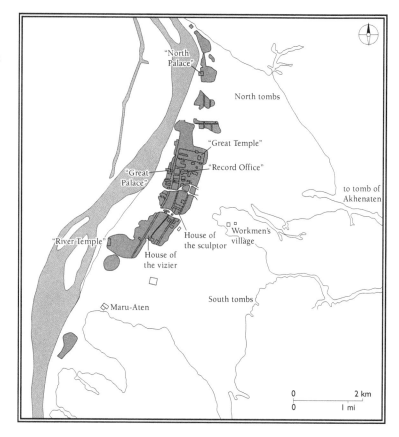

1. Why do you think the site of Amarna, a "semicircle of [limestone] cliffs on an isolated strip of land," appealed to Akhenaten?

_____

2. What were some advantages of this site for Egypt's capital city? For example, what building materials were nearby?

_____

3. What were some disadvantages of the site?

_____

4. The authors state that workers rode donkeys to "commute" into the city. Use the scale on the map to calculate the distance from the workmen's village to the following locations: the North Palace, the Great Temple, the Great Palace.

_____

5. How did the Great Temple at Amarna differ from older temples to the gods?

_____

NAME **DATE**

A. MULTIPLE CHOICE

Circle the letter of the best answer to each question.

1. Which of the following statements does **not** describe Akhenaten?
   a. He was devoted to his wife, Nefertiti.
   b. He believed in worshipping many gods.
   c. He was devoted to one god, Aten.
   d. He neglected Egypt.

2. Akhenaten broke tradition by
   a. living with his wife.
   b. sharing power with his wife.
   c. building temples.
   d. writing poems.

3. Akhenaten upset his subjects by announcing that
   a. he was going to leave Egypt.
   b. they could no longer live in Memphis.
   c. their cherished gods no longer existed.
   d. Nefertiti was going to be a priestess.

4. Akhenaten weakened the old priesthood by
   a. exiling them from Egypt.
   b. killing many of them.
   c. cutting off payments to them.
   d. not listening to their advice.

5. Akhenaten doomed his new religion to failure by
   a. building the city of Amarna.
   b. collecting taxes.
   c. marrying Nefertiti.
   d. denying Egyptians the afterlife.

B. SHORT ANSWER

Write one or two sentences to answer each question.

6. Where did Akhenaten build his new city for the god Aten?

_____

_____

7. How did the new temple at Amarna differ from older temples?

_____

_____

8. Why did Akhenaten build a university in Amarna?

_____

_____

C. ESSAY

Using information from the chapter, write an essay on a separate sheet of paper telling how Akhenaten "forgot Egypt" during his reign.

Chapter 16 Only Tomb Will Tell: Tutankhamen
Chapter 17 Surviving Childhood: Growing Up in Ancient Egypt
Chapter 18 War and Peace: Ramesses II and the Battle of Qadesh

UNIT OBJECTIVES

Unit 5 focuses on the years 1333–1274 BCE and on two famous rulers, Tutankhamen and Ramesses II. The unit includes a chapter about children in ancient Egypt—their health, toys, pets, and schooling. In this unit your students will learn

- ▶ the significance of the discovery of the tomb and mummy of Tutankhamen.
- ▶ what life was like for children in ancient Egypt.
- ▶ fact and fiction about Ramesses II and the Egyptian armies at the Battle of Qadesh.

PRIMARY SOURCES

Unit 5 includes pictures of artifacts/excerpts from the following primary sources:

- ▶ Howard Carter, diary entries
- ▶ Tutankhamen, Valley of the Kings, 1325 BCE
- ▶ Strabo, *Geography*
- ▶ Berlin Papyrus
- ▶ Delivery sayings
- ▶ Prophecy
- ▶ Princess Ahori registration declaration
- ▶ New Kingdom scribal advice, "The Instructions of Ani"
- ▶ Healing spell
- ▶ Traditional scribal advice, Papyrus Anastasi V
- ▶ Song of the Harpist
- ▶ Royal inscriptions, Qadesh battle inscriptions of Ramesses II

BIG IDEAS IN UNIT 5

Discovery, childhood, and **conflict** are the big ideas in Unit 5. The unit opens with Howard Carter's monumental discovery of the tomb and mummy of Tutankhamen (King Tut). The excavation of King Tut's tomb points up the limitations of the technology available to Carter. Next the unit looks at childhood in ancient Egypt. It was short (girls and boys usually married in their early teens) and perilous due to widespread disease. Schooling was available only for the privileged, but even the poorest children had toys. Finally, the unit explores conflict between the Egyptians and Hittites, specifically the battle of Qadesh as told by Ramesses II through inscriptions on his tomb.

Introduce these ideas by eliciting what students know about King Tut. Lead students to making accurate statements about King Tut, correcting assumptions, and pointing out that he was only 18 when he died.

GEOGRAPHY CONNECTION

Refer students to the map on page 129 and discuss the extent of the Egyptian empire under Ramesses II. Lead students to understand how the map reinforces the statement on page 128 that "whoever controlled Qadesh controlled the trade route from the coast."

TIMELINE

1333–1325 BCE	Reign of Tutankhamen, the "boy king"
1293–1185 BCE	Dynasty 19
1279–1212 BCE	Reign of Ramesses II
1274 BCE	Ramesses II fights Hittites in Battle of Qadesh

UNIT PROJECTS

Interviewing Howard Carter

Have students write and perform a skit portraying a press conference announcing Carter's discovery of Tutankhamen's tomb and mummy. One group of students can play newspaper reporters, another Howard Carter and his associates. To create the questions and answers, students can use information in Chapter 16 and in books and online sources.

Rules of the Game: Senet

Students can research Senet, the ancient Egyptian board game, and present an explanation of the rules to the class. They can create their own Senet board and playing pieces and teach the class how to play. One of several websites explaining the game is *www.gamecabinet.com/history/Senet.html*.

Mapping the Battle of Qadesh

Have students create an illustrated presentation showing actions of the Hittite and Egyptian armies at the Battle of Qadesh. Students can find clearly labeled maps showing the respective movements of the Egyptians and Hittites as well as an explanation of the action at *www.touregypt.net/featurestories/kadesh.htm*.

Investigating Abu Simbel

Divide the class into small groups to prepare illustrated presentations about the Abu Simbel temples of Ramesses II and his wife. These massive structures were moved between 1964 and 1968 when construction of the Aswan High Dam threatened them with submersion. Individual students can report on the following topics related to moving the temples: financing the move, the engineering challenges of moving and reconstructing the temples on higher ground, and their current status. Students can find information at *www.touregypt.net/abusimbel.htm*, recommended in the Websites section of their book.

ADDITIONAL ASSESSMENT

For Unit 5, divide the class into groups and have them all undertake the Investigating Abu Simbel project so you can assess their understanding of the significance of the reign of Ramesses II. Use the scoring rubric at the back of this guide to assess students' work, and have students rate their own work with the self-assessment rubric.

LITERATURE CONNECTION

The biblical story of *Exodus* tells of Moses and the Jewish exodus from Egypt. Numerous stories have been based on this biblical event. Disney's animated film *The Prince of Egypt* (1998) is loosely based on this story. In addition, suggest these works of fiction written by contemporary authors:

▶ Rubalcaba, Jill. *A Place in the Sun*. New York: Puffin Books, 1998. In this fictional tale, a 9-year-old boy is forced into a lifetime of hard labor in the gold mines of Nubia during the 13th century BCE.

▶ Henty, G. A. *The Cat of Bubastes: A Tale of Ancient Egypt*. Dover Publications, 2002. This adventure tale set in 1250 BCE recounts how a young prince named Amuba finds friendship in the house of an Egyptian high priest. The story incorporates details about everyday Egyptian life.

▶ Sonia Levitin. *Escape from Egypt*. New York: Puffin, 1996. This book retells the Exodus story.

▶ Green, Roger Lancelyn. *Tales of Ancient Egypt*. Puffin Books, 1996. This book retells the myths of ancient Egypt for young readers.

UNIVERSAL ACCESS

The following strategies are designed to cover a range of learning styles and reading, language, and skill levels.

Reading Strategies

▶ To facilitate reading, have students preview the artwork and captions in each chapter to make predictions about the content.

▶ Chapter 17 deals with several subtopics under the general topic of childhood. Have students create main idea statements for each subtopic. Then have them point out details or examples that support the main ideas.

▶ Have students read aloud sections of Chapter 18 about the Battle of Qadesh and then act out the movements of the armies to better understand what happened.

Writing Strategies

▶ Have students write a diary entry from the point of view of an observer who was with Howard Carter when he uncovered Tutankhamen's mummy. The entry should describe the excitement of the discovery and include specific details from Chapter 16.

▶ Ask students to write a short essay explaining the statement on page 122, "No one in the ancient world loved their children more than the Egyptians." Have students provide supporting details from the chapter.

Listening and Speaking Strategies

▶ Have two groups of students debate the question, Was Tutankhamen murdered? They can use evidence from Chapter 16 and other sources.

▶ Assign groups of students different chapters of Unit 5. Challenge them to become specialized museum tour guides (docents) for the King Tut, Childhood in Ancient Egypt, and Battle of Qadesh rooms in the museum. Students can do additional research beyond the chapter to learn more about their assigned room. Tour guides can then make presentations to the class explaining highlights of their site and encouraging the audience to visit.

UNIT VOCABULARY LIST

The following words that appear in Unit 5 are important for your students' understanding of the social studies content as well as for development of literacy. Use these words for vocabulary study or to reinforce language arts skills (e.g., synonyms, compound words, prefixes and suffixes, and related words). The words are listed below in the order in which they appear in the chapters.

Chapter 16	Chapter 17	Chapter 18
restoration	boomerang	insignificant
replica	anxious	vile
medley	fastidious	infantrymen
sentinel	pendant	vanquish
antechamber	pneumonia	interrogated
torso	descendants	rendezvous
tuberculosis	frenzied	isolated
vertebrae		infiltrated
fiber-optic		plundering
parasites		reinforcements
		stragglers
		truce

ONLY TOMB WILL TELL: TUTANKHAMEN

PAGES 115–121

CAST OF CHARACTERS

Tutankhamen (toot-an-KAH-mun) king of Egypt during Dynasty 18; best known as the "boy king"; his tomb, filled with fabulous treasures, was discovered by British archaeologist Howard Carter in 1922

THEN and NOW

A CT scan of Tutankamen's mummy conducted by the Egyptian Museum revealed that the king was not murdered, as many had suspected. Have students write a journal entry expressing their view of the importance of knowing how King Tut died.

VOCABULARY

sarcophagus A coffin made of stone

CHAPTER SUMMARY

In the 1920s Howard Carter discovered the tomb of Tutankhamen, whose father was probably the despised Pharaoh Akhenaten. Although the tomb had been broken into in the past, numerous artifacts still remained, including the pharaoh's solid-gold coffin.

PERFORMANCE OBJECTIVES

▶ To understand the effort involved in excavating Tutankhamen's tomb
▶ To recognize the significance of the treasures buried with Tutankhamen
▶ To summarize the achievements of Tutankhamen's short reign

BUILDING BACKGROUND

Invite students to share their ideas about buried treasure. Ask: Why is the idea of finding treasure buried in the earth so appealing? Explain that the tomb of Tutankhamen, excavated in the 1920s, revealed one of the greatest collections of buried treasure ever found.

WORKING WITH PRIMARY SOURCES

Encourage students to read aloud Howard Carter's diary entries in this chapter. Encourage interested students to read more about the discovery from Carter's point of view in his book, *The Discovery of the Tomb of Tutankhamen* (reprinted by Dover, 1977).

GEOGRAPHY CONNECTION

Location Have students access the Theban Mapping project (*www.thebanmappingproject.com*) to pinpoint the location of King Tut's tomb (number 62) in the Valley of the Kings. The site includes an interactive display of all of the tombs found in the valley. Students can use this to help them visualize the excavation of King Tut's tomb.

READING COMPREHENSION QUESTIONS

1. How did Howard Carter know that he had found the tomb of Tutankhamen? (*The king's cartouche [nameplate] was on the seals of the tomb.*)
2. Why is it important to have a photographic record of a tomb's contents? (*Some artifacts are so fragile that simply touching them causes them to disintegrate. A photograph can then be the only proof that something existed.*)
3. What reasons did others have for killing Tutankhamen? (*to become ruler; to steal his wife*)
4. What treasures were found in the tomb? (*chariots, statues, beds, game boards, pottery, shrine, coffins*)
5. Distribute copies of the blackline master for Chapter 16 so students can review the sequence of events that led to the discovery of Tutankhamen's tomb and mummy.

CRITICAL THINKING QUESTIONS

1. Why did Carter fear that tomb robbers had already opened and robbed Tutankhamen's tomb? (*He saw evidence that the doorway to the anteroom had been opened and reclosed previously.*)
2. What surprised Carter most in Tutankhamen's tomb? (*Students' responses will vary. He was surprised that tomb robbers had not succeeded in robbing the tomb after they broke in; he was also surprised about the solid-gold third coffin.*)
3. Why do you think Carter threw away an embalming tool found in the tomb? (*Responses will vary. Students should recognize that he didn't realize that later generations would have the technology to investigate the tool.*)

SOCIAL SCIENCES

Science, Technology, and Society   Invite a group of students to investigate the fiber-optic technology that allows archaeologists to examine a mummy without damaging it. Have the group report back to the class with an illustrated presentation.

READING AND LANGUAGE ARTS

Reading Nonfiction   Help students notice the progression of description in the chapter: from the outside of the tomb to the antechamber to the small inner tomb to the caskets to the body of Tutankhamen himself.

Using Language   Point out the words *seal* and *sealed* in Carter's diary entry for November 26 (page 117). Discuss the different meanings for the noun and verb *seal*, and lead students to appreciate the homonyms *sealing/ceiling*.

SUPPORTING LEARNING

English Language Learners   Have partners write descriptions of what Carter found in King Tut's sarcophagus, starting from the opening of the outer sarcophagus to the opening of the inner one.

Struggling Readers   Have students use the sequence of events chart in the back of this guide to show the steps in Carter's excavation of Tutankhamen's tomb. When they have completed their charts, have students evaluate the outcome of Carter's efforts.

EXTENDING LEARNING

Enrichment   Have students find illustrations of the treasures of Tutankhamen's tomb in books or online. Have students discuss what use King Tut would have had for each item in the afterlife.

Extension   Invite students to write and act out skits based on the following scenes from the chapter: the decision to look into the anteroom; the decision to "unstick" the mummy; the mystery of King Tut's death.

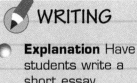

WRITING

- **Explanation** Have students write a short essay explaining the statement at the end of the chapter that "the dead do tell tales" with reference to the mummy of Tutankhamen.

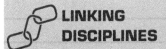

LINKING DISCIPLINES

Health Have students find out more about the effects on people today of the parasites described in the sidebar on page 119.

DISCOVERING TUTANKHAMEN

Directions

Place the events in the chart in the proper sequence by writing the letters of the events in the left-hand column in the order in which they happened. Then follow the instructions below.

Sequence	Events
1.	**A.** Lifting the lid of the solid-gold coffin
2.	**B.** Opening the doorway to a room full of "strange and beautiful" objects
3.	**C.** Lifting the lid of the sarcophagus
4.	**D.** Clearing the anteroom
5.	**E.** Opening the four shrines
6.	**F.** Finding Tutankhamen's cartouche (his mark)
7.	**G.** Discovering the mummy was stuck inside the coffin
8.	**H.** Uncovering the first step of an ancient stairway
9.	**I.** Cutting up Tutankhamen's mummy
10.	**J.** Entering the burial chamber

Write a short essay agreeing or disagreeing with the following statement: *Damaging Tutankhamen's mummy was a small price to pay for the tale it had to tell to investigators.*

_____

_____

_____

_____

_____

_____

_____

NAME   **DATE**

A. MULTIPLE CHOICE

Circle the letter of the best answer to each question.

1. The antechamber to King Tut's tomb was filled with
   a. things the king would need in the afterlife.
   b. limestone chips.
   c. mummies.
   d. precious jewels and gold.

2. The flowers found inside Tutankhamen's coffin identify the date of his burial as
   a. January.
   b. March.
   c. July.
   d. September.

3. Some information about Tutankhamen was lost because
   a. his mummy was partially destroyed when it was taken out of his coffin.
   b. water had seeped into his coffin.
   c. scientists were not interested in him.
   d. reaching his tomb was too difficult.

4. Tutankhamen's second coffin was unusually heavy because it
   a. was made out of stone.
   b. was full of water.
   c. had a solid-gold coffin inside it.
   d. was so old.

5. Tutankhamen's body was ruined when it was removed from its coffin because archaeologists of that time
   a. were not careful excavators.
   b. did not care about mummies.
   c. dropped the coffin.
   d. worked in terrible conditions.

B. SHORT ANSWER

Write one or two sentences to answer each question.

6. Why was everything in King Tut's tomb photographed before it was moved?

_____

_____

7. Why did it take a year to clear the antechamber in King Tut's tomb?

_____

_____

8. What could modern scientists have been able to tell Carter if they had been able to study King Tut when he was first discovered?

_____

_____

C. ESSAY

Write an essay on a separate sheet of paper telling about what happened during Tutankhamen's reign. Include information about the challenges the new king faced and how he and his advisors dealt with them.

FOR HOMEWORK

STUDENT STUDY GUIDE

pages 43–44

CAST OF CHARACTERS

Strabo (STRAY-bow) Greek geographer who wrote *Geographia*, a description of the world as known in his time

THEN and NOW

In ancient Egypt cats rated higher than dogs as pets. In the 21st century cats in the Western world are more popular than dogs for the first time since the days of the pharaohs. Have a group of students do an informal survey of the popularity of cats versus dogs at your school and graph the results.

CHAPTER SUMMARY

Ancient Egyptians loved their children. This chapter takes us from birth through childhood illnesses (and defenses against them) to toys, pets, and finally schooling. Childhood was short; most ancient Egyptians were married by the time they reached their early teens.

PERFORMANCE OBJECTIVES

▶ To understand how children were treated in ancient Egypt
▶ To explain the impact of the desert on the health of ancient Egyptians
▶ To compare education in ancient Egypt to education today

BUILDING BACKGROUND

Discuss with students their favorite toys from childhood. Then introduce this chapter by saying that Egyptian children also enjoyed toys. Read aloud the scribe's advice in the chapter's last sentence: "And do not tire of playing!"

WORKING WITH PRIMARY SOURCES

Ask students to read aloud the excerpts from "The Instructions of Ani" on page 124. Then ask them to create an instruction of their own about how children should treat their parents.

GEOGRAPHY CONNECTION

Region   Have a group of students investigate the physical characteristics of Egypt's desert region and prepare an oral report on its average rainfall, its plants and animals, and how its environment affects human health.

READING COMPREHENSION QUESTIONS

1. How did the Egyptians treat their children? (*They loved them, and raised all who were born. Children were considered a blessing. Pregnant women were fussed over, and Egyptian men were loving fathers.*)

2. Why did Egyptians hurry to name their children? (*Only those who had been named had the possibility of an afterlife. Because so many children died soon after birth, the parents named them as early as possible.*)

3. How did Egyptians try to protect their children from disease? (*Breast-feeding protected the children from parasites. They also used amulets and spells.*)

4. What did Egyptian children do for fun? (*They played hockey, tug-of-war, catch, board games, and with dolls and other toys. Most families had pets to play with.*)

5. Distribute copies of the blackline master for Chapter 17 to help students organize information from the chapter.

CRITICAL THINKING QUESTIONS

1. Do you agree with Strabo that the Egyptians' most admirable quality was "bringing up all the children that are born"? (*Responses will vary but should reflect an understanding that Strabo was Greek, and the Greeks killed unwanted infants, while we in the 21st century expect that parents will bring up all their children.*)

2. Why are the remains of an ancient Egyptian peasant boy valuable to scientists today? (*The dried-out remains of the peasant boy include the oldest intact brain yet found; his internal organs are in place and his heart is attached to his rib cage. Scientists have analyzed his remains to learn more about the health of ancient Egyptians.*)

3. Compare and contrast the ancient Egyptian style of learning with the style of learning in modern schools. (*Answers will vary, but students should recognize that some of the features of ancient Egypt schools are duplicated in their schools.*)

SOCIAL SCIENCES

Science, Technology, and Society   Have students investigate the modern technology that allows scientists to study mummified remains. Students can display their findings on a poster.

READING AND LANGUAGE ARTS

Reading Nonfiction   This chapter is organized by topics. Elicit the main topic (*childhood in ancient Egypt*) and ask students to identify the subtopics.

Using Language   Review with students the passage on page 127 describing the education of Egyptian children. Have students analyze the description to discover the words and phrases that create strong images.

SUPPORTING LEARNING

English Language Learners   Form small groups and have students tell about pets they have or had or would like to have, and what their favorite toys were when they were younger.

Struggling Readers   Have students complete the Venn diagram with the graphic organizers in the back of this guide to better understand the differences and similarities between Egyptian childhoods and their own.

EXTENDING LEARNING

Enrichment   Invite students to learn more about ancient Egyptian toys and games. They can examine pictures of them online at *http://nefertiti.iwebland.com/timelines/topics/games.htm*, recommended in the "Websites" section of the student book. Have students make a catalog of ancient toys and games with descriptive notes about each one.

Extension   Have students draw an outline of a human body and add arrows to indicate the location of Nakht's health problems. Students should label each problem. They can post their drawings on a bulletin board.

WRITING

Composition
Remind students that Egyptians had a favorite story about cats chasing Egypt's enemies away (page 126). Have students write their own two-page story from the point of view of a brave cat who helped to save Egypt.

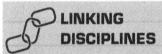

LINKING DISCIPLINES

Health Have interested students research the causes and modern treatment of either black lung disease or desert lung disease. They can then prepare a report for the class.

NAME _____ DATE _____

CHARTING CHILDHOOD

Directions

Column 1 lists topics about Egyptian childhood discussed in Chapter 17. Use column 2 to take notes about each topic as you read the chapter. Then complete the writing assignment.

Topic	Ancient Egyptian Children
Pets	
Toys	
Education	
Protection from Disease	

Choose one of the topics. On another sheet of paper, write a description of your experience with the topic. Then write another short essay comparing your experience to that of an ancient Egyptian child.

NAME _____ **DATE** _____

A. MULTIPLE CHOICE

Circle the letter of the best answer to each question.

1. Which of the following was **not** a way that ancient Egyptian parents treated their children?
 a. Children were welcomed into the world.
 b. Children were protected from harm by amulets.
 c. Unwanted children were left outside to die.
 d. Children were given toys and pets to play with.

2. What protected very young children from diseases of the digestive system?
 a. They drank only boiled water.
 b. They wore amulets.
 c. They were breast-fed by their mothers.
 d. They were rarely taken outdoors.

3. Which statement about education in ancient Egypt is correct?
 a. All children were required to go to school until they were 12.
 b. Only girls were educated.
 c. Education was available only to a few children.
 d. Education began at about 10 years old.

4. Which of the following conditions did **not** bother Nakht, the peasant boy?
 a. grains of dust in his lungs
 b. worms in his intestines
 c. cancer
 d. malaria

5. Which of the following animals were the most beloved pets in ancient Egypt?
 a. cats
 b. dogs
 c. horses
 d. donkeys

B. SHORT ANSWER

Write one or two sentences to answer each question.

6. Why is Nakht so important for the study of health of children in ancient Egypt?
 _____
 _____

7. Why does the chapter say that Nakht was always short of breath?
 _____
 _____

8. How did most Egyptian children spend their days?
 _____
 _____

C. ESSAY

On a separate sheet of paper, write an essay describing the life of a peasant child in ancient Egypt.

WAR AND PEACE: RAMESSES II AND THE BATTLE OF QADESH PAGES 128–134

CAST OF CHARACTERS

Ramesses (RAM-ah-seas) **II** or **Ramesses the Great** king of Egypt; fought against the Hittites; possibly king during the Israelite exodus; ruled for nearly 70 years

THEN and NOW

The Egyptian government reported in 2004 that workers on a construction project in Upper Egypt had uncovered an enormous limestone statue of a seated Ramesses II towering 39 feet high. Have students compare the height of this new discovery to that of the statues at Abu Simbel.

CHAPTER SUMMARY

The Battle of Qadesh between the ancient Egyptians and the Hittites was fought for control of an important coastal trade route. Ramesses II (Ramesses the Great) was the Egyptian pharaoh who took the fight to the Hittites and inscribed his tomb with accounts of the battle—some factual, some fabricated. In the treaty that ended hostilities, the Egyptian and Hittite kings promised to aid each other in the event of attack.

PERFORMANCE OBJECTIVES

▶ To understand the sequence of events in the Battle of Qadesh
▶ To analyze the movement of armies in the Battle of Qadesh through maps
▶ To understand that Ramesses's account of what happened in the battle may not be reliable

BUILDING BACKGROUND

Discuss with students the all-too-human habit of exaggerating to make oneself more important. Elicit examples of people who were caught exaggerating their accomplishments. Explain that the pharaoh Ramesses II inscribed an exaggerated report in stone and it has been read for generations afterward.

WORKING WITH PRIMARY SOURCES

Refer students to Ramesses II's Qadesh Battle Inscriptions in *The World in Ancient Times Primary Source and Reference Guide* for a closer look at the way in which he described his role in the battle. Have students identify specific instances of hyperbole and exaggeration. Then have them interpret what probably happened.

GEOGRAPHY CONNECTION

Location Direct students to the map on page 129. Discuss why the location of Qadesh made it important in controlling trade. Have students refer to the map in answering such questions as these: Why would Egypt want to control Qadesh? Why would the Hittites want to control it?

READING COMPREHENSION QUESTIONS

1. How was Ramesses tricked by the Hittites on the eve of battle? (*Two captured "deserters" from the Hittites told Ramesses the Hittite army was far away; in fact, it was nearby and ready to attack.*)
2. In the treaty of peace, what did the Hittite and Egyptian kings agree to do? (*If either king were attacked and asked for help, the other king would send troops "and chariots" to help.*)
3. When he wrote on his tomb, "Behold, I am victorious, me alone!" what was Ramesses talking about? (*He was describing how he single-handedly defeated the Hittites who surprised him in his camp at Qadesh.*)
4. Distribute copies of the blackline master for Chapter 18, which asks students to interpret diagrams of the Battle of Qadesh.

CRITICAL THINKING QUESTIONS

1. How did Akhenaten's failings in foreign relations affect Egypt in the time of Ramesses II? (*Akhenaten had ignored the Hittite threat in Syria, and the Hittites increased their power there. By the time of Ramesses II, the Hittites had taken over a critical trade route, forcing Egypt to act.*)

2. Why did the Hittites fail to defeat the Egyptians they ambushed? (*The Hittites were distracted by stealing from the Egyptians and were attacked by Egyptian reinforcements.*)

3. Why is Ramesses' version of how peace talks came about probably an exaggeration? (*Since the Hittites kept control of Qadesh, it is unlikely that the Hittite king begged for a truce as Ramesses claimed.*)

SOCIAL SCIENCES

Science, Technology, and Society   Have students investigate how the Abu Simbel statues were moved when the Aswan Dam was built. They can start their research at *www.touregypt.net/featurestories/abusimbel.htm*, recommended in the Websites section of their book.

READING AND LANGUAGE ARTS

Reading Nonfiction   Have students read the extracts from the peace treaty and note the use of ellipses and single quotation marks. Discuss the conventions of using ellipses within quotations as a way to indicate words that have been omitted, double quotes for quoted material and single quotes for quotations within a quotation.

Using Language   The first page of the chapter contains two powerful similes. Have students locate the similes ("like the snout of a barking dog" and "like locusts in their numbers") and discuss their meaning.

SUPPORTING LEARNING

Struggling Readers   Have students complete the sequence of events chart in the back of this guide to aid in understanding the Battle of Qadesh and the movements of the Egyptian and Hittite armies.

EXTENDING LEARNING

Enrichment   The Great Temple at Abu Simbel was relocated to higher ground in the 1960s. Have students research current concerns about ancient structures in the Valley of the Kings. Students can use the Theban Mapping Project website listed in the Websites section at the back of their book: *www.thebanmappingproject.com*.

Extension   Divide students into two groups to debate this question: Was Ramesses II truly "The Great"? Have the two groups present arguments pro and con and the remainder of the class vote to decide which argument was the more effective.

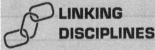

LINKING DISCIPLINES

Art Have students locate and copy pictures of the Abu Simbel statues of Ramesses II in books or online at *www.touregypt. net/featurestories/abusi mbel.htm*. Have students make a collage of the pictures.

WRITING

News Article Have students take the role of reporters traveling with the Egyptian army and write a news article about an event during the Battle of Qadesh. Remind them to answer the questions *Who? What? When? Where? Why? How?*

NAME _____   **DATE** _____

THE BATTLE OF QADESH

Directions

Study the three diagrams below of the Battle of Qadesh. Then pick an appropriate caption for each diagram from the choices below, and write the caption below each diagram.

Scene 1 _____

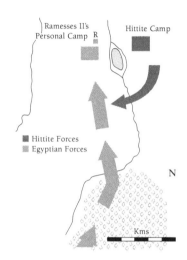

Caption: _____

Scene 2 _____

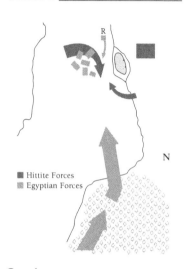

Caption: _____

Scene 3 _____

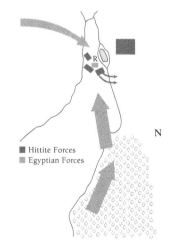

Caption: _____

Caption Choices

A. Mass Confusion

B. Reinforcements Save the Day

C. Egypt Retreats

D. Surprise Attack

NAME _____ **DATE** _____

A. MULTIPLE CHOICE

Circle the letter of the best answer to each question.

1. Which of the following is **not** a reason for the battle of Qadesh?
   a. Egypt wanted to take over the Hittite empire.
   b. Egypt wanted control over the trade route from the coast.
   c. Egypt wanted to control the Mediterranean.
   d. Egypt had to defend the Nile Delta from Hittite attack.

2. Qadesh was
   a. a fortified city in Hatti.
   b. a small city in the Wood of Labwi.
   c. a large city on the Mediterranean Sea.
   d. an island-city in the Orontes River.

3. What led to the Hittite ambush of Ramesses at Qadesh?
   a. Ramesses trusted a false report that the Hittite army was far away.
   b. Ramesses refused to remain safely in back of the army.
   c. Ramesses men assured him he was safe.
   d. Ramesses was busy preparing for a surprise attack of his own.

4. Although Ramesses claimed to have won the battle single-handed, the truth is that
   a. Ramesses had help from his shield bearer.
   b. Egyptian reinforcements saved the day.
   c. Ramesses was killed in the battle.
   d. the Hittites captured Ramesses.

5. The ultimate outcome of the Battle of Qadesh was that Egypt and Hatti
   a. fought each other for years.
   b. destroyed Qadesh.
   c. merged into one empire.
   d. negotiated a peace treaty.

B. SHORT ANSWER

Write one or two sentences to answer each question.

6. Why did Ramesses II have to battle the Hittites?

   _____

   _____

7. Why didn't the Hittites capture Ramesses at Qadesh?

   _____

   _____

8. Why didn't the Battle of Qadesh decide things between Egypt and Hatti?

   _____

   _____

C. ESSAY

Ramesses II was known as Ramesses the Great. Based on information in the Chapter 18, write an essay on a separate sheet of paper discussing whether he was truly a great leader.

THE THIRD INTERMEDIATE PERIOD

Chapter 19 Scratch and Sniff: Village Life
Chapter 20 Battle Stations: The Sea Peoples
Chapter 21 Happily Ever After: The Arts
Chapter 22 King for a Day: Kush, Nubia, and the Third Intermediate Period

UNIT OBJECTIVES

Unit 6 covers the topics of village life, the arts, and two powerful rulers, the latter during the years 1207–575 BCE, a time of invasion and foreign rule. In this unit your students will learn

- ▶ how the rulers Ramesses III and King Piye of Kush rescued Egypt—one from the invading Sea Peoples and the other from internal warfare.
- ▶ what life was like in the village of Deir el-Medina.
- ▶ the ancient Egyptian story of Rhodopis, a version of the Cinderella story.

PRIMARY SOURCES

Unit 6 includes pictures of artifacts/excerpts from the following primary sources:

- ▶ Ebers Papyrus
- ▶ Oath taken in court, court documents
- ▶ Notes on ostraca (broken pottery with notes written on it) found at Deir el-Medina
- ▶ Inscriptions from Ramesses III's mortuary temple
- ▶ Strabo, Egyptian story of Cinderella
- ▶ *The Tale of Wenamun*
- ▶ Stela of Piye

BIG IDEAS IN UNIT 6

Lifestyle, conflict, and **diversity** are the big ideas of Unit 6. Insights into the lifestyles of workmen and their families are revealed in artifacts found in the village of Deir el-Medina. Egyptians' art, like their lifestyles, was subject to strict rules. The unit discusses conflict between Egyptians and invaders as well as conflict between forces within Egypt. Diversity came to Egypt with foreign invaders—the Sea Peoples and the Kushite King Piye, whose goal was not domination but reunification of Upper and Lower Egypt.

Elicit that the lives of common people are often overlooked in histories of the ancient world because records kept then usually focused on the lives and actions of rulers and other powerful people. What we know about the lives of ordinary people often comes from other sources—archaeological evidence such as the ostraca found at Deir el-Medina.

GEOGRAPHY CONNECTION

The movement of people into Egypt is important for understanding the events in this unit. Refer students to the map on page 76 so they can see why Ramesses III had the upper hand in his battles with the invading Sea Peoples. Refer students to the map on page 151 to trace the movements of King Piye of Kush.

TIMELINE

1207 BCE	First attack of the Sea Peoples
1182–1151 BCE	Reign of Ramesses III
1174 BCE	Ramesses III defeats the Sea Peoples
1070 BCE	Third Intermediate Period begins
747 BCE	Reign of King Piye; Nubian/Kushite Dynasty begins

UNIT PROJECTS

Modeling an Egyptian House

Invite students to make a model of a workman's house in the village at Deir el-Medina. They can find details about the layout of the house in Chapter 19. As the basis for a model they can find a diagram and dimensions at *www.reshafim. org.il/ad/egypt/building/deir_el_medine.htm*. When completed, students can label parts of the model to identify how each part of the house was used.

Military Strategy

Ramesses III's defeat of the Sea Peoples was an extraordinary victory. Have volunteers research the course of the battle and the strategies of the opponents. They can draw diagrams of the battle's beginning, middle, and end, showing the successful Egyptian strategy. The diagrams should be labeled, have a legend and a distance scale, and use symbols to represent the opposing forces.

Artwork

Invite students to "paint like an Egyptian." Have students create pictures of people using the ancient Egyptian style. They can find outlines of paintings to trace or color at one of the websites recommended in the Websites section in their book: *www.guardians.net*. (Students should go to the Kids Section and then to Color Me Egypt and read the instructions.) They can also download art to color at *www.clevelandart.org/kids/egypt/color/index.html*, the website of the Cleveland Museum of Art.

Guidebook for Kush

Have a group of students research information about the kingdom of Kush. Group members can collect information in the following categories: rulers, people, achievements, art, architecture, economy, and geography. They can consult library/media center and online sources and present the completed guidebook to the class.

ADDITIONAL ASSESSMENT

For Unit 6, divide the class into groups and have them all undertake the Guidebook for Kush project so you can assess their understanding of the location of Kush and its political, commercial, and cultural relations with Egypt. Use the scoring rubric at the back of this guide to assess students' work, and have students rate their own work with the self-assessment rubric. Be sure to distribute the library/media center research log (see rubric at the back of this guide) to help students evaluate their sources as they conduct their research.

LITERATURE CONNECTION

The Greek geographer Strabo's *Geographica*, a description of the world as he knew it, is available in translation. Read some passages aloud to the class, and discuss with them how the climate and geography of Egypt impressed the writer. A guide to the Stela of Piye and other Egyptian texts is available on-line at *http://www.touregypt.net/sitemap.htm.*

UNIVERSAL ACCESS

The following strategies are designed to cover a range of learning styles and reading, language, and skill levels.

Reading Strategies

▶ Have students use the K-W-L graphic organizer at the back of this guide to assist them in their reading. Preview each chapter, and have students write what they *know* about the subject. Have them write what they *want to know* about the subject in the second column. When they are finished with the chapter, have them complete the third column by writing what they *learned.*

▶ Chapters 19 and 21 deal with two or three subjects apiece. Assist students in defining those subjects, and have them create main idea statements for each. Then have them point out details or examples that support the main ideas.

▶ Have groups of four students read this unit, one chapter per student. Each group member should take notes on the reading. Group members should come together to tell each other what they learned about Deir el-Medina, Ramesses III, Egyptian art, and King Piye of Kush.

Writing Strategies

▶ Have partners make a three-column chart with headings for each of the unit's big ideas. Partners should get together after reading each chapter to jot down their observations in each category.

▶ Have students make an idea web, using *village lifestyle* as the central circle. They can fill in the outer circles with details about lifestyles of people in the workmen's village, Deir el-Medina.

Listening and Speaking Strategies

▶ To spark students' interest, read aloud the title and first paragraph of each chapter. Use the reading as a springboard for predicting what the chapter is about. Record and review students' predictions. When students have finished reading the chapter, ask whether their predictions were correct.

► Encourage small groups of students to prepare dramatic readings of sections of a chapter or of extracts from the primary sources used in the chapter. They might use props or actions to help dramatize the events. The group can present their dramatization to the class.

UNIT VOCABULARY LIST

The following words that appear in Unit 6 are important for your students' understanding of the social studies content as well as for development of literacy. Use these words for vocabulary study or to reinforce language arts skills (e.g., synonyms, compound words, prefixes and suffixes, and related words). The words are listed below in the order in which they appear in the chapters.

Chapter 19	Chapter 20	Chapter 21	Chapter 22
conveniences	deployed	frontalism	nomadic
accumulate	ragamuffins	innovator	earnest
incense	desperate	mural	contempt
frankincense	horde	sacred ratio	legitimate
myrrh	slaughter	galaxy	heir
willy-nilly	surrender	proportion	coalition
repel	whirlwind	percussion	valiant
niche	volley	reveler	battering ram
barter	maneuver	gyrating	grievous
company town	grappling hooks		compassionate
honeycomb	capsize		
floodplain			
toting			
plummet			
tunic			

SCRATCH AND SNIFF: VILLAGE LIFE

PAGES 135–140

THEN and **NOW**

During the last decade, the Theban Mapping Project (TMP) has measured tombs in the Valley of the Kings in order to generate 3-D computer models. Students can visit the Valley of the Kings on the TMP website: *www.thebanmapping project.com.*

LINKING DISCIPLINES

Math Challenge students to calculate how much water each of the six state-supplied water carriers delivered every day to homes in Deir el-Medina. Using information from page 139 (68 homes with 6 people per home; 4 gallons per person), have students calculate the weight of the water carried by each water carrier each day (1 gallon of water weighs 8.33 pounds).

CHAPTER SUMMARY

Notes written on scraps of broken pottery (ostraca) in the village of Deir el-Medina offer archaeologists invaluable insights into village life in ancient Egypt. The workers who lived in the village built the tombs in the Valley of the Kings. Despite heat, insects, and unhealthful living conditions, the people showed a lively interest in trade, work, and each other.

PERFORMANCE OBJECTIVES

▶ To understand the layout of an ancient Egyptian village and home
▶ To recognize the importance of the information provided by the ostraca found at Deir el-Medina
▶ To contrast ancient Egyptian villagers' possessions and level of sanitation with our own

BUILDING BACKGROUND

Have students create a list of their top five favorite possessions. Then ask them how many of those items might have existed in ancient Egypt. Explain that in Chapter 19 they will enter an ancient Egyptian working-class home.

WORKING WITH PRIMARY SOURCES

Refer students to Letters from Deir el-Medina in *The World in Ancient Times Primary Sources and Reference Volume* for more insights into the lives of the people who lived in the village and worked in the Valley of the Kings. Have students select a letter and read it aloud expressively to a small group.

GEOGRAPHY CONNECTION

Location   On a map of Egypt have students locate Thebes, the Valley of the Kings, and Deir el-Medina. Ask students to estimate the distance from the village to the Valley of the Kings. Invite interested students to learn more about the geology of the Valley of the Kings and report to the class about the advantages of its location.

READING COMPREHENSION QUESTIONS

1. How were the homes in Deir el-Medina constructed? (*They were built from mud bricks.*)
2. Where did the residents of Deir el-Medina usually sleep, and why? (*They usually slept on the roof, where it was cooler.*)
3. How did people in Deir el-Medina get things they needed? (*They bartered and used sacks of grain as cash.*)
4. How do we know the kinds of things they bartered with and for? (*They kept records and wrote notes on broken pottery pieces called ostraca that have been discovered and translated.*)
5. Distribute copies of the blackline master for Chapter 19. Have students complete the chart and the writing assignment.

CRITICAL THINKING QUESTIONS

1. What is an advantage and a disadvantage of building a home out of mud bricks? (*The advantage: mud is plentiful and cheap; the house is easy to rebuild; the disadvantage: the house crumbles over time and has to be rebuilt.*)

2. What do the authors mean when they say Deir el-Medina was a "company town"? (*The people who lived there all worked in the same place [Valley of the Kings necropolis] and had some services, like laundry, provided by the employer/state.*)

3. Why was the back of the house considered undesirable? (*It was where the kitchen and oven were located, so it was hot and unpleasant in hot weather.*)

4. How do we know so much about the people who lived in Deir-el-Medina? (*We know about them from notes written on pottery and thrown away in a dry well, where they were preserved.*)

SOCIAL SCIENCES

Science, Technology, and Society   Have students make a flow chart showing the steps in brick making described on page 135. Have them create an additional flow chart showing the steps involved in building a new house on the same spot where an old house has collapsed.

READING AND LANGUAGE ARTS

Reading Nonfiction   Have students identify the topics of village life covered in this chapter (sewers, construction, layout, and contents of houses, the necropolis, water access, ostraca). Have students identify these sections and give the main idea and details for each.

Using Language   Have students identify the words at the beginning of the chapter that describe unpleasant smells and sights. Then ask them to identify the part of speech of each word and use the words in original sentences.

SUPPORTING LEARNING

Struggling Readers   Have students use the outline graphic organizer at the back of this guide to organize the main ideas and details related to life in Deir el-Medina.

EXTENDING LEARNING

Enrichment   Invite a group of students to research the details of a dispute between workers at Deir el-Medina and Ramesses III. They can find information at *www.touregypt.net/featurestories/medina.htm*. Have students present the dispute in the form of a problem/solution presentation to the class.

Extension   Ask volunteers to read aloud their diary entries describing life in Deir el-Medina (see the blackline master) and the persuasive ostraca they composed for the Writing assignment. They can also read aloud actual ostraca selections from the chapter and from Letters from Deir el-Medina in *The World in Ancient Times Primary Sources and Reference Volume.*

VOCABULARY

necropolis a city for the dead (a large number of tombs)

WRITING

○ **Persuasion** Using a sheet of paper, write a 150-word ostraca, a short note proposing the terms for the sale,
○ rental, lending, or borrowing of a bicycle (the 21st-century equivalent of a donkey). Use complete sentences.

AT HOME IN DEIR EL-MEDINA

Directions

Listed below in column 2 are some things found in homes in Deir el-Medina. First list sections of the house in the spaces in column 1. (Use information from Chapter 19.) Then put the letter of each item in column 2 in the correct "room" (column 1) and describe what the item was used for (column 3). Finally, complete the writing assignment below.

Sections of House	Items Found Inside Home	Used For
	A. griddle stones	
	B. woven mat	
	C. wood for the fire	
	D. 26 onions	
	E. oven	
	F. beds	
	G. 2 folding stools	
	H. statues of gods	

On a separate sheet of paper write a short diary entry from the point of view of a visitor to the busy village of Deir el-Medina. Explain who lives in the village and where they work. Using complete sentences and information from the chapter, describe what you liked and didn't like about the village.

NAME   **DATE**

A. MULTIPLE CHOICE

Circle the letter of the best answer to each question.

1. Which of the following was **not** a part of a home in Deir el-Medina?
   a. entrance hall
   b. banquet room
   c. kitchen
   d. niche for the gods' statues

2. Which of the following best describes the streets of Deir el-Medina?
   a. wide and shaded
   b. narrow and clean
   c. dusty and quiet
   d. smelly and unhealthy

3. The inhabitants of Deir el-Medina were
   a. skilled tomb builders and their families.
   b. slaves and their masters.
   c. scribes and their families.
   d. royal servants and their families.

4. The deep well that the residents of Deir el-Medina tried to dig was important to archaeologists'
   understanding of the village because
   a. people were later buried in the well.
   b. the residents threw their garbage into the well.
   c. it made excavating nearby tombs easier.
   d. it showed how people worked together.

5. Which of the following adjectives best describe a home in Deir-el-Medina?
   a. dark and airless
   b. spacious and airy
   c. tiny and cool
   d. large and dark

B. SHORT ANSWER

Write one or two sentences to answer each question.

6. What did the residents of Deir el-Medina use as the foundation of their homes?

7. What was the layout of the typical house in Deir el-Medina?

8. What did the residents of Deir el-Medina do to keep bugs and pests away?

C. ESSAY

Write an essay on a separate sheet of paper comparing and contrasting living conditions in Deir el-Medina with conditions in a modern American town.

CAST OF CHARACTERS

Ramesses (RAM-ah-seas) **III** king of Egypt; successfully defended the country against invading Sea Peoples

THEN and NOW

The Ramesses dynastic name went on until Ramesses XI, but historians say that the greatness of the Ramesses pharaohs ended with Ramesses III. Discuss "dynasties" students are likely to be familiar with, such as the Kennedy or Bush families in American politics.

CHAPTER SUMMARY

Under Ramesses III, Egyptians successfully defeated the invading Sea Peoples on land and sea. The decisive battle took place in narrow waterways at the mouth of the Nile. Egyptian ships using oars outmaneuvered the Sea Peoples' sailing ships. Ramesses III took credit for the decisive victory by inscribing its details on the wall of his mortuary temple.

PERFORMANCE OBJECTIVES

▶ To summarize the threat posed by the Sea Peoples
▶ To understand how Ramesses III used temple inscriptions to promote his prowess in battle
▶ To describe how Egyptians fought the Sea Peoples on land and on water

BUILDING BACKGROUND

Ask students to describe famous movie monsters that cause everyone in their path to tremble with fear. Explain that the Sea Peoples were the monsters of Ramesses III's time. No one was able to stop them, and they were headed straight for Egypt!

WORKING WITH PRIMARY SOURCES

Have students read the text of Ramesses III's temple inscriptions and discuss their reliability as historical evidence. Ask: What other record of events could balance Ramesses III's version of history? (*an independent account from a writer who was not Egyptian or otherwise related to Ramesses*)

GEOGRAPHY CONNECTION

Movement   Distribute copies of the blackline master for Chapter 20. Have students follow directions for completing the map and discussing the battle.

READING COMPREHENSION QUESTIONS

1. From which direction did the Sea Peoples approach Egypt? (*northeast*)
2. Why did the Egyptians fear the Sea Peoples? (*They had the reputation of destroying everything in their path.*)
3. Although the Egyptians were not a seafaring people, what advantage did they have over the Sea Peoples on water? (*The Egyptian ships were powered by oars and were thus more maneuverable in the narrow waterways of the Nile Delta than the Sea Peoples' sail-powered boats.*)
4. How did Ramesses defeat the Sea Peoples? (*His army stood firm against the onslaught on land. His navy herded the Sea Peoples' boats closer to shore, where the Egyptian archers could reach them with volleys of arrows.*)

CRITICAL THINKING QUESTIONS

1. Draw conclusions about what the Sea Peoples' army depended on to defeat other armies. (*According to the description of the battle, the Sea Peoples depended on overwhelming numbers and mass charges to sweep away their enemies.*)

2. Summarize how Ramesses III boosted his image as a powerful leader. (*by having scenes of himself triumphing over enemies carved on walls of temples; by inscribing monuments with accounts of his heroism*)

3. When leaders want to boost their image, why do they often brag about military victories? (*Success in battle makes a leader seem strong and decisive, especially if the battle helps protect the people the leaders are trying to impress.*)

SOCIAL SCIENCES

Science, Technology, and Society   Have a group of students find out more about the warships used by Ramesses III and why they prevailed against the Sea Peoples at *www.touregypt.net/featurestories/navy.htm*. Have students download images and create an illustrated presentation of the topic.

READING AND LANGUAGE ARTS

Reading Nonfiction   While they read, have students use the cause and effect chart at the back of this guide to identify the causes and effects of Egypt's victory over the Sea Peoples.

Using Language   Have students identify the verbs and verb forms used in the first two paragraphs of the chapter. Ask them to define any that are unfamiliar and then assess how effective the verbs are at setting the mood for the chapter opening.

SUPPORTING LEARNING

English Language Learners   Have students work in small groups to define the words used to describe the Sea Peoples: *pirates, bandits, ragamuffins, motley*. After defining the words, ask students to use them in original sentences.

Struggling Readers   Ask students to use the sequence of events chart at the back of this guide while they read so they can keep track of events in Ramesses III's fight against the Sea Peoples.

EXTENDING LEARNING

Enrichment   Have a group of students investigate the Sea Peoples. They can find information online at *http://nefertiti.iwebland.com/sea_peoples.htm*. The group can report back to the class about the various theories of who the Sea Peoples were.

Extension   Have one group of students play the roles of some of the Sea Peoples' leaders and explain why they are invading Egypt. Have another group play the roles of Ramesses III and his advisers, who explain why the Sea Peoples must be kept out of Egypt.

WRITING

Composition Ask students to imagine they are one of Ramesses III's subjects who has visited his temple and read the inscriptions about the battle with the Sea Peoples. Have students write a diary entry describing what they saw and read and what they think of Ramesses III as a result.

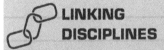

LINKING DISCIPLINES

Art Have students draw a picture of one of the scenes described on page 143. Ask students to label their drawings and display them in class.

THE SEA PEOPLES VERSUS RAMESSES III

Directions

Complete the map using the steps below. Then complete the writing assignment.

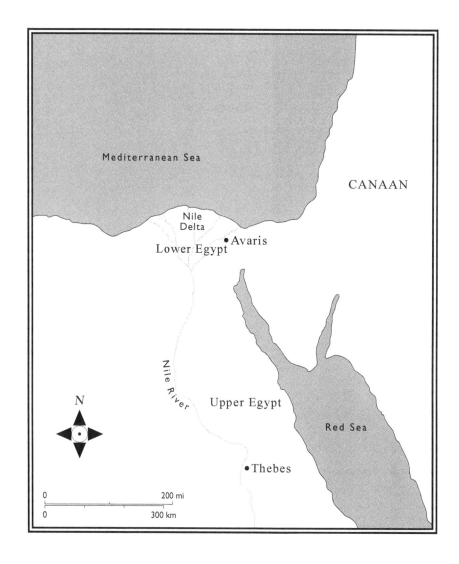

1. Draw red arrows to show the direction from which the Sea Peoples came to Egypt by land.

2. Draw a green line to show the defensive stand that Ramesses III made against the army of the Sea Peoples.

3. Label the Nile Delta. Draw ships in the Delta: red for the Sea Peoples', green for the Egyptians'. Include the important features of the boats that allowed the Egyptians to win the sea battle.

4. On a separate sheet of paper, write a short description of what happened in the battle with the Sea Peoples.

A. MULTIPLE CHOICE

Circle the letter of the best answer to each question.

1. The Egyptians feared the Sea Peoples, who had
   a. destroyed powerful kingdoms elsewhere.
   b. already invaded Egypt.
   c. demanded tribute from Egypt.
   d. lived in Egypt for years.

2. The Sea Peoples attacked Egypt by
   a. land from the south.
   b. sea from the north.
   c. land and sea from the west.
   d. land and sea from the northeast.

3. The Egyptian army defeated the Sea Peoples' army because it
   a. had more advanced weapons.
   b. kept perfect alignment against the chaos of the attack.
   c. outnumbered them two to one.
   d. staged a surprise attack.

5. Ramesses III inscribed descriptions of battle on his temple walls in order to
   a. appear as a powerful leader.
   b. give his stone carvers a job.
   c. frighten the Sea Peoples.
   d. improve the looks of the temple wall.

4. The Egyptian navy was victorious because
   a. its sailors were better than the Sea Peoples' sailors.
   b. its boats were much larger than those of the Sea Peoples.
   c. it trapped the navy of the Sea Peoples in the narrow river mouths.
   d. the Sea Peoples ran out of arrows.

B. SHORT ANSWER

Write one or two sentences to answer each question.

6. Why did Ramesses III want to fight the Sea Peoples before they got to Egypt?

7. How would the outcome of the battle have been different if the two navies had fought out in the Mediterranean Sea?

8. What techniques did the Egyptian navy use to defeat the navy of the Sea Peoples?

C. ESSAY

The chapter states "*Ma'at* had conquered chaos" after the battle against the Sea Peoples. Using details from the chapter, write an essay on a separate sheet of paper that explains this statement.

HAPPILY EVER AFTER: THE ARTS

PAGES 145–149

THEN and NOW

Variations on the Cinderella story exist in many cultures around the world. A popular modern version is told in *Ella Enchanted*, a book by Gail Carson Levine (HarperCollins, 1997), and in a motion picture of the same name (2004). Invite interested students to write a book or movie review of *Ella Enchanted*, paying particular attention to the credibility of characters, and share their reviews with the class.

WRITING

Composition Have pairs of students write an original scene for a Cinderella story set in modern times.

CHAPTER SUMMARY

The distinctive characteristics of Egyptian painting and sculpture were carefully maintained by artists' strict adherence to rigid rules. As an example of Egyptian influence on other civilizations, the chapter includes the story of the music-loving Rhodopis, a forerunner of Cinderella.

PERFORMANCE OBJECTIVES

► To describe some of the characteristics of Egyptian art
► To understand the significance of phi, the "sacred ratio"
► To recognize the common themes in the stories of Rhodopis and Cinderella

BUILDING BACKGROUND

Ask students what a credit card or a driver's license and Egyptian tombs have in common. Both are examples of the sacred ratio of length to width: 1.6180339 or phi. You can measure the credit card to show its proportions are approximately the same as phi. Then explain that the builder of Egyptian tombs had to use the sacred ratio in the tomb's proportions so that people buried in the tomb could reach the afterlife.

WORKING WITH PRIMARY SOURCES

Distribute copies of the blackline master for Chapter 21. Have students write their own versions of the dialogue based on the Rhodopis story told in the chapter.

GEOGRAPHY CONNECTION

Region   The story of Rhodopis takes place along the Nile River. Have students investigate the Nile Valley as a region in ancient times and today. They can note the characteristics that distinguish the Nile Valley from other parts of Egypt and the changes in the Nile Valley that have occurred since the Aswan Dam was completed in 1970.

READING COMPREHENSION QUESTIONS

1. What rule did Egyptian artists follow when painting important people? (*The important person had to be larger than anyone else in the picture.*)
2. What were some ancient Egyptian beliefs about paintings? (*A painting of a person was as good as a body for the journey to the afterlife.*)
3. Why was the sacred ratio important in building Egyptian tombs? (*Egyptians believed that if tombs were not built using phi, people buried there would not be able to go on to the afterlife.*)
4. Why were some Egyptian artists called "scribes of outlines"? (*They drew the outline of objects in a painting. A second person filled in the color.*)
5. How does Rhodopis express her love of music and dance in the story? (*She sings and dances for her animal friends.*)

CRITICAL THINKING QUESTIONS

1. An important theme in Egyptian art is pleasing the gods. Explain how the sacred ratio is an example of that. (*The gods were pleased by the sacred ratio, so any painting or sculpture or tomb that incorporated it pleased the gods.*)

2. What do the authors mean when they say Egyptian artists "were more craftsmen than innovators"? (*Artists followed age-old rules about how to paint and did beautiful work, but they did not experiment with new ways of depicting the world.*)

3. Besides the location of the story, what is a major difference between the Cinderella and Rhodopis stories? (*Students may mention that Cinderella's glass slippers are gilded slippers in Rhodopis's story; Cinderella's stepsisters and prince are Rhodopis's servant girls and king; Rhodopis's "fairy godmother" is a raven.*)

SOCIAL SCIENCES

Science, Technology, and Society   Have students find out more about the use of phi, the sacred ratio, in Egyptian art. To see examples of Egyptian art, refer students to *www.touregypt.net/featurestories/artoverview.htm*.

READING AND LANGUAGE ARTS

Reading Nonfiction   Have students notice the place in the text where ancient Egyptian music and dance are discussed. Ask: What is surprising about the placement of this information?) (*It comes in the third paragraph of the Rhodopis story.*) Discuss whether the informational paragraph interrupts the story or fits in naturally.

Using Language   Point out the colloquialisms *stay within the lines* and *happily ever after* and discuss their meanings. Have students use them in original sentences with their modern meanings.

SUPPORTING LEARNING

English Language Learners   Have students work in pairs identifying the musical instruments mentioned on page 148. Have students locate pictures or actual instruments to connect with the words.

Struggling Readers   Have students use a Venn diagram at the back of this guide to compare the Cinderella fairy tale and the Rhodopis story.

EXTENDING LEARNING

Enrichment   Have students find out more about the Cinderella story in other cultures. One source of information is the following site: *http://wneo.org/ WebQuests/TeacherWebQuests/Cinderella/The_Cinderella_Project.htm*. Have students create a written report of their findings.

Extension   Have students work in groups to create a play based on the Rhodopis story. They can use the dialogue they created on the blackline master, adding a narrator to explain parts of the story not covered by the dialogue.

LINKING DISCIPLINES

Music Have students investigate and report on ancient Egyptian music. They can find information online at *http://nefertiti. iwebland.com/timelines/ topics/music.htm*.

RHODOPIS: THE PLAY

Directions

Scenes from the Rhodopis story are listed below. For each scene add dialogue for the characters. Use information in Chapter 21 to create your dialogue.

Scene 1: Rhodopis and other servant girls at the home of an old Egyptian.

Servant Girl 1:

Servant Girl 2:

Servant Girl 3:

Rhodopis:

Scene 2: The old Egyptian gives Rhodopis fancy slippers.

Old Egyptian:

Rhodopis:

Servant Girls:

Scene 3: Rhodopis washes clothes in river as the other girls go to the king's party.

Servant Girls (calling from boat in river):

Hippo (after splashing mud on one of Rhodopis's slippers):

Rhodopis (washing slipper):

Falcon (grabbing slipper):

Scene 4: The king's party

King (after the Falcon drops slipper at his feet):

Scene 5: The king comes looking for the girl who can wear the slipper.

King:

Servant Girls:

King to Rhodopis (hiding in the rushes):

Rhodopis (pulling the other slipper from under her tunic):

All: And they lived happily ever after!

NAME   **DATE**

A. MULTIPLE CHOICE

Circle the letter of the best answer to each question.

1. Which of the following is **not** a characteristic of ancient Egyptian art?
  a. Crocodiles and other dangerous animals were drawn with spears sticking in them.
  b. Important people were painted larger than anyone else in the picture.
  c. Artists made sure the subject's arms and legs were in the picture.
  d. The artist's signature was centered at the bottom of the painting.

2. Why would an Egyptian demand that a tomb be built in the proportions of the "sacred ratio"?
  a. to impress other Egyptians   **c.** to make sure of reaching the afterlife
  b. to follow the rules   **d.** to please the king

3. Frontalism is a style of art in which
  a. the head is drawn in profile and the body straight on.
  b. the body is drawn in profile and the head straight on.
  c. the entire body is drawn straight on.
  d. the entire body is drawn in profile.

4. What does Falcon do in the Rhodopis story?
  a. He pecks the mean servant girls.   **c.** He takes Rhodopis's slipper to the King.
  b. He splashes mud on the slipper.   **d.** He gives the slippers to Rhodopis.

5. Which of the following animals plays a part in the Rhodopis story as told in this chapter?
  a. Hippopotamus   **c.** Cat
  b. Leopard   **d.** Rhinoceros

B. SHORT ANSWER

Write one or two sentences to answer each question.
6. In your opinion, are artists less creative when they have to follow rules?

_____

_____

7. Why was the ratio Egyptian artists used called the "sacred ratio"?

_____

_____

8. Why does the main character of Rhodopis like music?

_____

_____

C. ESSAY

On a separate sheet of paper, write an essay summarizing the most important characteristics of ancient Egyptian art.

KING FOR A DAY: KUSH, NUBIA, AND THE THIRD INTERMEDIATE PERIOD

PAGES 150–156

STUDENT STUDY GUIDE

pages 53–54

CAST OF CHARACTERS

Piye (PEE-yee), also **Piankhi** (pee-AHNK-ee) king of Kush and then of Egypt; thought to be the first king of Dynasty 25

Wenamun (WEN-ah-mun) Egyptian character, possibly fictional; the story of his journey takes place at the end of the New Kingdom Period

THEN and NOW

King Piye is known by other names—Pianhki, Piyi—and titles: Men-Kheper-re (The Manifestation of Re Abides), and Sema-tawy (Uniter of Two Lands). Have students investigate the full, official names and titles of Great Britain's ruler, Queen Elizabeth II, and Prince Charles, her son. Invite students to create descriptive titles for themselves.

CHAPTER SUMMARY

Out of the chaos of the Third Intermediate Period, Egypt once more divided into two kingdoms—Upper and Lower Egypt. King Piye of Kush reunited Egypt once again and established a century of Kushite rule. The chapter includes *The Tale of Wenamun*, a parable of how low Egypt had sunk in the eyes of the world.

PERFORMANCE OBJECTIVES

▶ To understand the disorder of the Third Intermediate Period and Egypt's loss of standing in the world

▶ To calculate the significance of *The Tale of Wenamun* to Egypt's plight

▶ To summarize King Piye's contributions to Egypt

BUILDING BACKGROUND

Ask students which of these adjectives accurately describe gold: *valuable, ordinary, precious, beautiful, cheap, expensive.* Remind students how important gold was to Egyptians. Explain that Egypt did not have gold mines but the nearby nation of Kush did. Kush supplied gold to Egypt and became rich and strong in its own right.

WORKING WITH PRIMARY SOURCES

Refer students to King Piye's Victory Stele in *The World in Ancient Times Primary Sources and Reference Volume* for an account of his conquest of Memphis. Have volunteers read aloud the selections and then discuss the similarities to the inscriptions honoring Ramesses II and III in chapters 18 and 20.

GEOGRAPHY CONNECTION

Place   Have students turn to the map on page 151 and locate Upper and Lower Egypt and the kingdom of Kush. Then have them use the map scale to determine how far King Piye traveled to reach first Thebes and then Lower Egypt.

READING COMPREHENSION QUESTIONS

1. How did Kush become strong enough to save Egypt? (*Kush's gold mines made Kush strong.*)

2. In *The Tale of Wenamun*, why did the high priests send Wenamun outside of Egypt to buy timber, and how was he supposed to pay for it? (*Egypt did not have much timber; he was given gold and silver to pay for it.*)

3. Why did kings in Lower Egypt plan a rebellion? (*They resented having a Kushite ruler in Upper Egypt.*)

4. What delayed King Piye's attack on the north? (*He spent a month at the Opet Festival, a necessity if he wanted to be accepted as divine king of Egypt.*)

5. Distribute copies of the blackline master for Chapter 22 so students can review the sequence of events in King Piye's rescue of Egypt.

CRITICAL THINKING QUESTIONS

1. Why did King Piye describe himself this way: "every heart was heavy with fear of him"? (*His army besieged and attacked towns and won battles.*)

2. What do you think was the result of King Piye's forgiving of the defeated kings of Lower Egypt? (*They were loyal to him and kept Egypt united.*)

3. Refer students to the "Report of Wenamun," an excerpt from *The Tale of Wenamun* in *The World in Ancient Times Primary Sources and Reference Volume.* Help students make the connection that Wenamun's treatment in this excerpt symbolizes Egypt's standing in the world at the time.

SOCIAL SCIENCES

Civics   Have students make a flow chart of events in the chapter showing how Egypt moved from disunity to unity under King Piye. Ask students to evaluate King Piye as a ruler, listing his strengths and weaknesses.

READING AND LANGUAGE ARTS

Reading Nonfiction   Have students evaluate the authors' point of view about King Piye. For example, on page 150 the authors write that Piye *must have shaken his head sadly* and *did not like bloodshed.* Ask students to present other evidence in the chapter about the authors' feelings toward King Piye.

Using Language   Relate the name of the country—Nubia—to the name of the people who lived there—Nuba. Have students find another such relationship in the chapter: *Ethiope* and *Ethiopia.* (See A Rose by Any Other Name sidenote on page 148.) Ask students if they can think of any other countries or states with *-ia* at the end.

SUPPORTING LEARNING

Struggling Readers   Have students pair up to retell the story of Wenamun in their own words. Make sure students understand that the story symbolizes Egypt's weakness in the Third Intermediate Period.

EXTENDING LEARNING

Enrichment   Kush is identified with Nubia, Ethiopia, and Sudan. Ask a group of students to determine the location of Kush in ancient times and show its location on a map of the world. Then ask volunteers to report back to the class on current events in that area of the world.

Extension   Students can present a press conference held by King Piye after his return to Kush. Questions from reporters should touch on Piye's motivation for reuniting Egypt and for treating the defeated kings of Lower Egypt generously. Several students can take the role of King Piye.

WRITING

Persuasion Have students write a letter from King Piye to the rebellious kings in Lower Egypt explaining why a united Egypt would be stronger than a divided one.

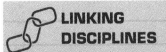

LINKING DISCIPLINES

Economics Have students analyze *The Tale of Wenamun* to discover insights into the Egyptian economy of the period. Ask: Who sends Wenamun on a journey? What valuables are in his possession? Why? What can you conclude about the economic power of the high priests at Karnak?

KING PIYE REUNITES UPPER AND LOWER EGYPT

Directions

Write the letter of each event in the correct order in column 1. Then explain the significance of each event, using complete sentences.

Correct Order	Event	Significance
1. _____	**A.** Piye decides his duty is to restore *ma'at* to Egypt.	
2. _____	**B.** Piye's army marches north; fights rebels on land and water and wins.	
3. _____	**C.** Piye sends his sister to rule Upper Egypt as wife of the god Amun.	
4. _____	**D.** Piye returns to Kush after reuniting Upper and Lower Egypt.	
5. _____	**E.** Piye forgives enemies.	
6. _____	**F.** Kings in Lower Egypt plan rebellion against Upper Egypt.	

NAME   **DATE**

A. MULTIPLE CHOICE

Circle the letter of the best answer to each question.

1. Which of the following is **not** a reason King Piye marched into Egypt?
   a. He wanted to unite Upper and Lower Egypt.
   b. He wanted to see his sister.
   c. He wanted to restore *ma'at* to Egypt.
   d. He wanted to rescue Egypt.

2. How does *The Tale of Wenamun* show that Egypt was weak?
   a. The King of Dor is rude to Wenamun when Wenamun reports a theft.
   b. Egypt has no timber, so Wenamun has to go to Dor to get some.
   c. The King of Dor refuses an offer of help from Wenamun.
   d. Wenamun has to travel alone on an important mission.

3. Which statement sums up the authors' view of King Piye?
   a. He cared about restoring Egypt to its position as a world power.
   b. He was bloodthirsty and cruel to his prisoners and horses.
   c. He cared about horses more than people.
   d. He wanted to steal Egypt's riches and return to Kush.

4. King Piye had to spend time at the Opet Festival in Karnak because
   a. he loved festivals.
   b. the rituals of the Opet Festival confirmed his right to rule Egypt.
   c. if he didn't, the flood waters might not go back into the Nile.
   d. he needed to build up his army for the fight in the north.

5. Which of the following statements best describes the priests of Karnak?
   a. They were not allowed to own land.   c. They were very poor.
   b. They marched into battle with King Piye.   d. They had a tight hold on Egypt's economy.

B. SHORT ANSWER

Write one or two sentences to answer each question.

6. Why had Egypt become so weak by the time of King Piye?

   _____

   _____

7. What was to be the fate of Egypt from the Third Intermediate Period onward?

   _____

   _____

8. What does Piye's instructions to his army to stop at the temple of Karnak and purify themselves show about the influence of religion in Egypt?

   _____

   _____

C. ESSAY

Using details from the chapter, write an essay on a separate sheet of paper summarizing King Piye's rescue of Egypt.

EGYPT, GREECE, AND ROME

Chapter 23 Great Expectations: The Greek Period
Chapter 24 The Last Chapter: Graeco-Roman Rule

UNIT OBJECTIVES

Unit 7 focuses on the years 332–330 BCE, the final acts in the history of ancient Egypt before it came under Roman rule. The unit explores the influence of Alexander the Great and the development of Alexandria under the Ptolemaic pharaohs and culminates in the reign of Cleopatra, one of the most familiar of Egyptian rulers. In this unit your students will learn

► Alexander the Great's impact on Egypt.
► the wonders of Alexandria, founded by Alexander the Great and developed by the Ptolemaic pharaohs, including the last, Cleopatra.
► Egypt's connection with Rome and the reign of the last pharaoh, Cleopatra.

PRIMARY SOURCES

Unit 7 includes pictures of artifacts/excerpts from the following primary sources:

► Plutarch, *Life of Alexander*
► Homer, the *Odyssey*
► Arrian, *Anabasis of Alexander*
► *Letter of Aristeas*
► Pliny the Elder, *Natural History*
► Inscription on the Pharos Lighthouse
► Plutarch, *Life of Antony*
► Shakespeare, *Antony and Cleopatra*
► Ptolemy, *Almagest*
► Galen, medical writings
► Heron, *Pneumatica*

BIG IDEAS IN UNIT 7

Change, power, and **learning** are the big ideas presented in Unit 7. The unit begins and ends with dramatic changes: from Alexander the Great's "invasion" of Egypt and founding of Alexandria, through the rule of the Ptolemaic pharaohs and the world-renowned changes they made to Alexandria to the change in Egypt's fortunes brought about by Cleopatra's ambitious connections with Rome. Alexander's power never diminished in his lifetime, but in the Roman Empire, Cleopatra met a power greater than hers. The period covered in this unit was a golden age of learning in Egypt, when Alexandria's library and museum were home to the world's greatest minds.

Introduce these ideas showing selected portions of DVD or VHS recordings of popular movies about Alexander and Cleopatra. After you have viewed these recordings, discuss students' impressions of the characters, and have them write them down. Then, ask them to compare these impressions with those they get from the historical narrative in the chapters.

Refer students to the map on page 159 showing the extent of Alexander's conquests—from Macedon to the border of India. On a map of ancient Egypt have students find the Siwah Oasis and calculate how far into the desert Alexander traveled to consult the oracle. A map of ancient Alexandria showing the presumed location of the library and museum would also be useful.

TIMELINE

332 BCE	Alexander the Great invades Egypt; Hellenistic Period begins
3rd century BCE	Manetho, Egyptian priest and historian, first divides Egypt's history and pharaohs into dynasties
305 BCE	Ptolemaic dynasty begins in Egypt with Ptolemy I
285–246 BCE	Reign of Ptolemy II; builds great lighthouse at Pharos and establishes library at Alexandria
51–30 BCE	Reign of Cleopatra, last of the Ptolemaic dynasty
30 BCE	Cleopatra dies; Hellenistic Period ends; Roman rule begins

UNIT PROJECTS

Alexander the Great's Death

Invite students to research the circumstances of Alexander the Great's death and theories about its cause. Students can find a summary of theories, including one that suggests he might have died of West Nile virus, on the U.S. government's Centers for Disease Control website at *www.cdc.gov/ncidod/EID/vol9no12/03-0288.htm*. Ask students to work together to prepare an oral problem-and-solution report on the topic.

Alexandria Underwater

Invite students to find out about and report on underwater archaeological explorations of Alexandria, the recovery of underwater artifacts, including what are believed to be stones from the Pharos lighthouse, and the feasibility of an underwater museum. Students can find information about the lighthouse at Pharos at the UNESCO website: *www.unesco.org/csi/pub/papers2/alex6.htm#pharos* and the feasibility of an underwater museum at *www.unesco.org/csi/pub/papers2/alex8.htm#feasibility*.

Cleopatra's Guided Tour of the Museum in Alexandria

Ask students to write and present a script for Cleopatra's visit to the Museum at Alexandria. Guides from the museum can explain what's going on in different sections of the museum, based on information in Chapter 23. Cleopatra's questions should indicate her interest in expanding the museum.

Chronology

Have students research the major events in Cleopatra's life. Then they can create a chronology chart annotated with comments about the significance of each major event.

ADDITIONAL ASSESSMENT

For Unit 7, divide the class into groups and have them all undertake the Cleopatra's Guided Tour of the Museum in Alexandria project so you can assess their understanding of the wonders and influence of Alexandria. Use the scoring rubric at the back of this guide to assess students' work, and have students rate their own work with the self-assessment rubric. Be sure to distribute the library/media center research log (see rubric at the back of this guide) to help students evaluate their sources as they conduct their research.

LITERATURE CONNECTION

Most of the records from this time come from Greek and Roman poets and historians, such as Plutarch, Homer, and Pliny the Elder (among others). Many stories have been based upon the historical accounts of Plutarch, such as *Life of Alexander* (79 CE) and *Life of Antony* (110 CE). In fact, Shakespeare's play *Antony and Cleopatra* is loosely based on Plutarch's account of Mark Antony's life.

Suggest the following works of historical fiction to students who want to learn more about this period. (You might want to advise students that historical fiction is not always accurate in its details.)

▶ Gregory, Kristiana. *Cleopatra VII: Daughter of the Nile, Egypt, 57 B.C.* Scholastic, 1999. A fictionalized diary of Cleopatra's tumultuous life as the young Queen of Egypt.

▶ Shakespeare, William. *Antony and Cleopatra.* Various editions of Shakespeare's dramatic retelling of the love between the Egyptian queen and the Roman military leader, Mark Antony, are available; it is perhaps one of the better-known plays by Shakespeare.

UNIVERSAL ACCESS

The following strategies are designed to cover a range of learning styles and reading, language, and skill levels.

Reading Strategies

▶ Have partners read the text together. Suggest that one student read a section aloud, then have the other paraphrase the reading.

▶ Before reading a chapter, point out potentially difficult words and ask volunteers to pronounce and define them. Say each word several times, then write it on the board. Help students associate the spoken word with the written word.

▶ Call on students to read sections of the chapters aloud, for example, the description of Alexander at Pharos and the site of the future city of Alexandria (pages 161–163). Encourage students to make their voices expressive and to use hand gestures where appropriate. Fit the reading passage to the abilities of each student.

Writing Strategies

▶ Have partners make a three-column chart with headings for each of the unit's big ideas. Partners should get together after reading each chapter to jot down their observations in each category.

▶ Let students create a visitors' guide to Alexandria in the time of Cleopatra, containing information about the library, museum, and lighthouse at Pharos. They can use information in the chapter and online resources to explain what visitors could expect to see.

▶ Have students make an idea web, using the big idea *learning* as the central circle. They can fill in the outer circles with details about the areas of learning that went on in Alexandria.

Listening and Speaking Strategies

▶ Encourage a group of students to prepare and present a "Person in the Street" interview involving a reporter for an Egyptian newspaper and a number of Alexander's trusted aides. The interviews can take place at Siwah Oasis. The reporter can ask the aides what they like about Alexander, why they have followed him as far as Egypt, what his plans are for Alexandria, and what he is doing out here in the desert.

▶ Have students make masks of the personalities in this unit, using paper plates and craft sticks. Call on volunteers to come to the front of the class and tell facts about their chosen personalities while holding their masks in front of their faces.

UNIT VOCABULARY LIST

The following words that appear in Unit 7 are important for your students' understanding of the social studies content as well as for development of literacy. Use these words for vocabulary study or to reinforce language arts skills (e.g., synonyms, compound words, prefixes and suffixes, and related words). The words are listed below in the order in which they appear in the chapters.

Chapter 23	**Chapter 24**
invincible	magnitude
unmanageable	smugglers
assassination	forfeit
destined	dowels
flanked	dabble
uplifting	intermission
coronation	gusto
omen	companionship
oracle	irresistible
dune	adjacent
	dissect
	anatomy
	autopsy
	stellar

GREAT EXPECTATIONS: THE GREEK PERIOD PAGES 157–163

CAST OF CHARACTERS

Alexander the Great king of Macedon; conquered Egypt and parts of Asia

Homer Greek poet; author of *The Iliad* and *The Odyssey*

Plutarch (PLOO-tark) Greek philosopher and biographer who wrote *Lives of the Noble Greeks and Romans*

THEN and NOW

Two scientists recently used a computer program to diagnose Alexander's last illness. Along with other symptoms, the fact that ravens dropped dead in Babylon the day he marched in suggested to them that West Nile virus might have caused his death. Since Alexander's remains have never been found, it is impossible to know for sure. Have interested students research and report to the class on the spread of West Nile virus in the United States.

CHAPTER SUMMARY

Alexander the Great was hailed by the Egyptians, who were grateful that he had saved them and their religion from Persian rule. During his six months in Egypt, Alexander designed a city, was proclaimed a god as well as the pharaoh, and consulted an oracle about his future. Though he never again returned to Egypt, his legacy was felt for centuries.

PERFORMANCE OBJECTIVES

▶ To understand why Egyptians felt appreciative toward Alexander the Great
▶ To describe Alexander's actions in Egypt
▶ To summarize Alexander's legacy in Egypt

BUILDING BACKGROUND

Ask students what images come to mind when they hear the name Alexander the Great. Remind them that movies about Alexander haven't always been accurate. Explain that in this chapter they are going to see him through the eyes of those who wrote about him long ago.

WORKING WITH PRIMARY SOURCES

Encourage students to read more of Plutarch's *Life of Alexander* online at *http://classics.mit.edu/Plutarch/alexandr.html*. Students can read selections from Plutarch aloud to the class. Based on these selections, help students draw conclusions about Plutarch's opinion of Alexander.

GEOGRAPHY CONNECTION

Movement Provide students with a map of Egypt (or use the one on page 159) that shows the Siwah Oasis. Have students confirm the distance from Alexandria to Siwah (300 miles) and trace Alexander's probable route as they read the account of his journey to the oracle (pages 162–163).

READING COMPREHENSION QUESTIONS

1. What were Alexander's accomplishments by the time he marched into Egypt? (*He ruled Macedon and Greece and had conquered ancient Turkey.*)
2. What impressed Alexander when he marched into Egypt on the way to Memphis? (*The temples and pyramids were the largest structures he had ever seen; he liked that they were built for the gods.*)
3. Why did Alexander go to Pharos, near the future site of Alexandria? (*He dreamed that Homer told him to go and possibly build a city there.*)
4. What happened when Alexander was pacing out the city of Alexandria? (*Birds ate the flour he had used to mark the site after his supply of chalk dust ran out.*)
5. What did Egyptian oracles typically tell people who asked them questions? (*whether or not the gods were pleased with them*)

CRITICAL THINKING QUESTIONS

1. What significant role did birds play during Alexander's time in Egypt? (*Birds ate the flour Alexander used to mark the future site of Alexandria, which led to a prediction that Alexandria would be the "feeder of all nations." Ravens showed Alexander the way to the oracle at the Siwah Oasis.*)

2. Do you think the difficulties of the journey to Siwah made advice from the oracle more or less valuable to people who came there? (*Students will probably say "more valuable" since people had paid a high price in the effort to get it.*)

3. Why do you think the authors say that Alexander "changed Egypt more than any other pharaoh"? (*Responses will vary. Students may say it was because he restored Egyptian religion and built Alexandria, or that because his world-famous name was now linked to Egypt, he brought Egypt to the world's attention.*)

SOCIAL SCIENCES

Civics   Have students make a two-column chart to compare the Persian rulers' views of Egyptian religion with Alexander's views. Ask them to include details from the chapter in the chart.

READING AND LANGUAGE ARTS

Reading Nonfiction   Have students use the sequence of events chart graphic organizer in the back of this guide to trace Alexander's activities in Egypt.

Using Language   Direct students to look at the first paragraph on page 158. Ask them to identify the pronouns in the paragraph and point out which pronouns identify the horse. Ask them to rewrite the information in a paragraph of their own, using pronouns correctly.

SUPPORTING LEARNING

English Language Learners   Invite volunteers to read aloud dramatic sections of the chapter: Alexander taming the horse; entering Egypt; dreaming of Homer and Pharos; planning the city of Alexandria; visiting the oracle.

Struggling Readers   Have students complete a main idea map graphic organizer at the back of this guide to create a character web for Alexander, placing his name in the middle and surrounding it with his character traits.

EXTENDING LEARNING

Enrichment   Have students locate images of Alexander the Great in books and online. Ask them to look closely at one of the images of Alexander and then write a character study based on what they can tell about Alexander from the artwork.

Extension   Have small groups dramatize one of the episodes of Alexander the Great's life as described in the chapter. One student can narrate the scene while the others act it out with appropriate dialogue.

WRITING

Composition
Remind students that Alexander's conversation with the oracle at the Siwah Oasis remains a mystery. Ask them to write a one-page dialogue in which Alexander introduces himself to the oracle and asks a question, and the oracle responds. By the end of the dialogue it should be clear why Alexander kept the oracle's words a secret. Have volunteers working in pairs read each other's dialogues aloud.

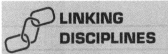

LINKING DISCIPLINES

Art Distribute copies of the blackline master for Chapter 23 and lead students in sketching their own city plan.

DESIGN YOUR CITY

When Alexander arrived at the site of the future Alexandria, he started at once to design the city. Use the space below to sketch out a city named for you!

Directions

In the space below write the name of your city and make a sketch showing some or all of the following:

- ▶ The location of major public buildings
- ▶ Streets (give them names)
- ▶ Areas where people will live, work, and play
- ▶ Waterfront with docks, lighthouse

- ▶ Bridges
- ▶ Roads leading in and out of your city
- ▶ A sewer system (Alexander thought of one for Alexandria)

Then, on another sheet of paper, answer these questions in complete sentences:

1. What is your city's motto?

2. What do you want your city to be known for?

Name of City: _____

NAME _____ **DATE** _____

A. MULTIPLE CHOICE

Circle the letter of the best answer to each question.

1. Which of the following is **not** one of the reasons Egyptians welcomed Alexander the Great, their conqueror?
   a. He ordered temples to be rebuilt.
   b. He looked like a god.
   c. He defeated the hated Persian rulers.
   d. He worshipped the god Amun

2. Alexander worshiped Amun as
   a. his father.
   b. the Egyptian representative of Zeus.
   c. the most powerful of gods.
   d. his ancestor.

3. Why did Alexander travel to Pharos?
   a. Alexander dreamed that Homer urged him to go to Pharos.
   b. Homer and Alexander had visited Pharos once and Alexander wanted to go again.
   c. Alexander planned to go to Pharos from the moment he entered Egypt.
   d. Alexander's seer told him it would be a good place for a city.

4. After birds ate the flour Alexander used to mark out the site of Alexandria, his seer told him that the city would
   a. not be a success.
   b. suffer drought and famine.
   c. feed many nations.
   d. be destroyed by another conqueror.

5. Alexander's mother and the people of Egypt seemed to agree that Alexander was
   a. not a good ruler.
   b. a god.
   c. a great father.
   d. a great priest.

B. SHORT ANSWER

Write one or two sentences to answer each question.

6. Explain why the Egyptians welcomed Alexander with cheers.

_____

_____

7. What made Pharos a good site for a port city?

_____

_____

8. What signs seemed to show that Alexander was divine on his trip to Siwah?

_____

_____

C. ESSAY

Using details from the chapter, write an essay on a separate sheet of paper explaining why Alexander deserved to be called "Great."

24

THE LAST CHAPTER: GRAECO-ROMAN RULE

PAGES 164–172

CAST OF CHARACTERS

Ptolemy (TALL-uh-mee) **I** Greek general under Alexander the Great; king of Egypt

Ptolemy II Greek king of Egypt best known for building the Lighthouse (Pharos) at Alexandria, one of the Seven Wonders of the Ancient World, and for establishing the Great Library at Alexandria

Sostrates (SAUCE-trah-tees) Greek architect best known for designing and building the great Lighthouse (Pharos) at Alexandria

Cleopatra VII queen of Egypt

Plutarch (PLOO-tark) Greek philosopher and biographer who wrote *Lives of the Noble Greeks and Romans*

CHAPTER SUMMARY

The Ptolemaic pharaohs, successors to Alexander the Great, ruled an increasingly chaotic Egypt. Alexandria, the seat of learning in the ancient world, was their jewel. Cleopatra, the last of the Ptolemies, played a dangerous game with the Romans. She lost, but not before attracting world-class thinkers to Alexandria.

PERFORMANCE OBJECTIVES

▶ To describe the glories of the city of Alexandria
▶ To recognize the significance of Cleopatra's dealings with Rome
▶ To understand the legacy of the scholars who made Alexandria great

BUILDING BACKGROUND

Talk with students about libraries; elicit their first visit to a library and what it means to have a library card. Explain that in this, the last chapter, they will learn about the greatest library the world has ever known.

WORKING WITH PRIMARY SOURCES

Have students read Plutarch's *Life of Antony* to see how Plutarch presents Cleopatra. Plutarch's *Lives* can be found online at *http://classics.mit.edu/Plutarch/ antony.html*. Have students read selections aloud and evaluate Plutarch's opinion of Cleopatra.

GEOGRAPHY CONNECTION

Place Provide students with maps of the ancient city of Alexandria and the modern city. You can find a map of the ancient city online at *http://ils.unc.edu/dpr/ path/alexandria/geography.htm*. Have students compare and contrast the two cities.

READING COMPREHENSION QUESTIONS

1. How do we know the Ptolemies loved learning and building? (*Ptolemy II built the Pharos Lighthouse; he also built the Great Library of Alexandria, filled it with books from all over the world, and invited scholars to come there.*)

2. How did the Romans become involved with Egypt? (*The Egyptian ruler, Ptolemy XII, needed help from Rome, and his promises to Rome threatened to bankrupt Egypt. When his subjects chased him from Rome, Ptolemy convinced the Romans to put him back in power. This started the Roman connection with Egypt.*)

3. Why did Cleopatra invite Julius Caesar and Mark Antony to Egypt? (*to show them how rich the Egyptians were; to get them to help her build an empire*)

4. What were some of the subjects being studied in Alexandria during Cleopatra's reign? (*physics, literature, medicine, astronomy, geography, philosophy, mathematics, biology, engineering*)

CRITICAL THINKING QUESTIONS

1. How do we know that Cleopatra loved knowledge? (*She expanded the Alexandria Museum and invited scholars to live there and exchange ideas.*)

2. Why is it significant that Cleopatra spoke Egyptian? (*She was the only Ptolemaic pharaoh in nine generations to speak the language of the people she ruled. It made her a better ruler, and helped her influence other people.*)

3. Which classroom in the Alexandria Museum would you most like to visit? Why? (*Students' responses will vary. Heron's robotics class would be a popular choice because it has applications in today's world and sounds like fun.*)

SOCIAL SCIENCES

Science, Technology, and Society   The beacon of the lighthouse at Pharos could be seen for miles. Have students find out more about the building of the lighthouse and the technology of the light and report their findings to the class.

READING AND LANGUAGE ARTS

Reading Nonfiction   Distribute copies of the blackline master for Chapter 24 to help students understand the convention of numbering years before the Common Era as BCE and after the Common Era as CE. Have students complete the blackline master and then find dates in the chapter—in captions, sidebars, and the box on page 170—and place them on the CE/BCE timeline.

Using Language   Direct students' attention to the last paragraph on page 168 and its continuation on page 169. Read the description aloud and then have students identify examples of alliteration. Some examples are *ooze opulence; fabric fluttered; steered, ship, silver; cupids, Cleopatra, couch, reclined; announced, arrival.* Then ask students to write sentences with alliterative words of their own choosing.

SUPPORTING LEARNING

English Language Learners   Have partners make a list of adjectives in the chapter, such as *stellar, bustling, irresistible,* and *spellbinding.* Students can define these words from context and use them in original sentences.

Struggling Readers   Have students use the outline graphic organizer in the back of this guide to organize the main ideas and details related to the greatness of Alexandria.

EXTENDING LEARNING

Enrichment   Invite students to research and report on the discovery of what archaeologists believe is the site of the Alexandria library. The BBC news website has the story: *http://news.bbc.co.uk/1/hi/sci/tech/3707641.stm.* Students can also investigate the modern library and antiquities museum in Alexandria at *www.touregypt.net/featurestories/alexmuseum.htm.*

Extension   Have students work in small groups to investigate each of the people on "Alexandria's Honor Roll" (page 170). Conclude with a "press conference" where each Honor Roll member explains his feeling about studying and working in Alexandria and answers questions posed by the class.

WRITING

Poetry Encourage students to think about a time when learning felt good—such as when learning to ride a bike, to read, to swim, to solve a math problem. Then ask them to write a four-to-six-line poem about how that experience of learning something felt to them. To get started, read aloud and discuss Ptolemy's poem on page 172.

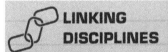

LINKING DISCIPLINES

Science and Mathematics Have students find out more about the discoveries, inventions, and legacies of the famous scientists and mathematicians— thinkers who lived, studied, and taught in ancient Alexandria— Ptolemy, Euclid, Heron, Galen, and Archimedes.

UNDERSTANDING BCE AND CE

Directions

Place the following dates in the correct spots on the Timeline below:

50 CE, 1750 BCE, 1250 CE, 200 BCE

Now write these century "names" of these centuries next to the first year of the century:

21st CE; 2nd BCE, 16th BCE, 6th CE, 21st BCE

Finally, in the space provided,

add the next year in the sequence for both CE and BCE

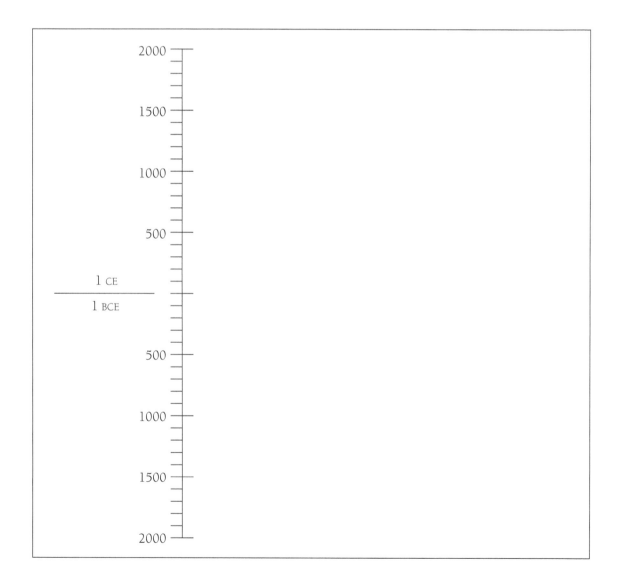

A. MULTIPLE CHOICE

Circle the letter of the best answer to each question.

1. Which of the following was **not** an achievement of Ptolemaic pharaohs who came after Alexander the Great?
   a. built the lighthouse at Pharos
   b. built the Great Library at Alexandria
   c. filled the library with books from all over the world
   d. built the Great Pyramid at Giza

2. Compared to the city of Rome, Alexandria was
   a. richer and more beautiful.
   b. a dirty slum.
   c. more foul-smelling.
   d. quiet and boring.

3. Which statement best describes Cleopatra?
   a. the most beautiful woman in the world
   b. a spellbinding, talented woman
   c. a quiet homebody
   d. a scholar who never left Alexandria

4. By the time of Cleopatra's rule approximately how many scrolls did the Great Library contain?
   a. 7,000
   b. 10,000
   c. 700,000
   d. 70,000

5. Which of the following would you probably **not** find in the Alexandria Museum in Cleopatra's time?
   a. zoos
   b. mummies
   c. scholars
   d. an observatory for stargazing

B. SHORT ANSWER

Write one or two sentences to answer each question.

6. What techniques were used to increase the number of books at the library in Alexandria?
   _____
   _____

7. What deal did Ptolemy XII strike with the Romans to keep his throne?
   _____
   _____

8. How did Ptolemy the astronomer change the maps of the world of that time?
   _____
   _____

C. ESSAY

On a separate sheet of paper, write an essay explaining this statement: "You don't need to wander into scholars' classrooms in Alexandria. They've wandered into yours." Use details from the chapter to support your main idea.

NAME   **DATE**

Directions

Answer each of the following questions on a separate sheet of paper unless directed to complete a chart on this page.

1. Draw a simplified map of the Nile Valley showing (a) the direction the Nile flows, (b) the modern name of the body of water the Nile flows into, and (c) the appearance of the Nile Delta. Then explain why the Nile was important to farmers. Use the words *nilometer* and *shaduf* in your answer.

2. The gods were important in every part of an ancient Egyptian's life. Explain the gods' connection to childbirth, the pharaoh, the Nile River, and the afterlife.

3. Like the other Egyptian pyramids, the Great Pyramid is an enormous structure that continues to impress visitors to Egypt today. Write a paragraph in which you discuss the purpose of the Great Pyramid, who worked on it, and the construction challenges they faced.

4. Describe the location of Kush in relation to Egypt. Then write a paragraph answering the following questions: What did Kush provide to Egypt through trade? What did King Piye of Kush contribute?

5. Use this idea web to describe the vizier in ancient Egypt. Tell who the viziers were, what their main responsibilities were, and why they were so powerful.

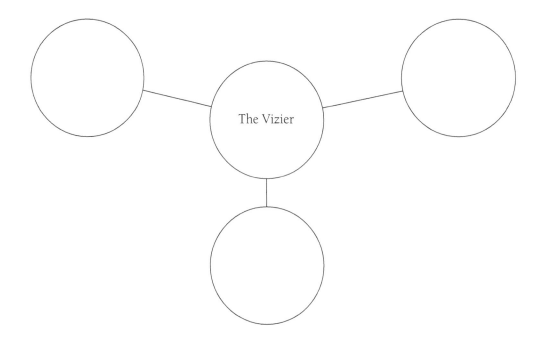

6. Write a sentence about each of the following explaining how they have contributed to historians' understanding of ancient Egypt: (a) Rosetta Stone, (b) Tomb of Tutankhamen, (c) ostraca at Deir el-Medina, (d) Amarna Letters.

7. First match each fictional character with his or her story by writing the correct letter from column 2 next to the character's name in column 1. Then, on a separate sheet of paper, write a sentence about why each story is important.

Character	Plot of Story
_____ **1.** Sinuhe	**A.** Huge serpent provides this character with gifts and predicts rescue on an island in the waves.
_____ **2.** Shipwrecked Sailor	**B.** Raven brings her slipper to the king. He starts looking for the girl who can wear it.
_____ **3.** Wenamun	**C.** He returns home after years as an exile—happy ending!
_____ **4.** Rhodopis	**D.** Robbed and helpless, this character is scorned by a foreign ruler.

8. Ancient Egyptian art is easy to recognize. Write two paragraphs: in the first paragraph describe the way people are portrayed in ancient Egyptian paintings; in the second describe some of the changes in Egyptian art during the Amarna Period.

9. Your book describes how waves of invaders changed ancient Egypt. In the chart, explain in full sentences what happened as a result of the invasions by each of the peoples listed.

Invader	Result
Hyksos	
Hittites	
Sea Peoples	

10. Link the ancient Egyptian rulers (column 2) with the important events/achievements of their reign (column 3). Write the letter of the achievement in column 1. Then choose one event and explain its importance in ancient Egyptian history.

	Ruler	Achievement
	1. Narmer	**A.** Defeats the Sea Peoples
	2. Djoser	**B.** Builds Great Pyramid at Giza
	3. Khufu (Cheops)	**C.** Builds Step Pyramid
	4. Hatshepsut	**D.** Supports Museum at Alexandria
	5. Akhenaten	**E.** First ruler to unite Upper and Lower Egypt
	6. Ramesses II	**F.** Sends expedition to Punt
	7. Ramesses III	**G.** Chooses site for Alexandria
	8. King Piye	**H.** Builds Amarna, a new capital city, and changes religion to worship of sun god
	9. Alexander the Great	**I.** Battles the Hittites; builds Abu Simbel temples
	10. Cleopatra	**J.** Unites Upper and Lower Egypt; rules from Kush

GRAPHIC ORGANIZERS

GUIDELINES

Reproducibles of seven different graphic organizers are provided on the following pages. These give your students a variety of ways to sort and order all the information they are receiving in this course. Use the organizers for homework assignments, classroom activities, tests, small group projects, and as ways to help the students take notes as they read.

1. Determine which graphic organizers work best for the content you are teaching. Some are useful for identifying main ideas and details; others work better for making comparisons, and so on.

2. Graphic organizers help students focus on the central points of the lesson while leaving out irrelevant details.

3. Use graphic organizers to give a visual picture of the key ideas you are teaching.

4. Graphic organizers can help students recall important information. Suggest students use them to study for tests.

5. Graphic organizers provide a visual way to show the connections between different content areas.

6. Graphic organizers can enliven traditional lesson plans and encourage greater interactivity within the classroom.

7. Apply graphic organizers to give students a concise, visual way to break down complex ideas.

8. Encourage students to use graphic organizers to identify patterns and clarify their ideas.

9. Graphic organizers stimulate creative thinking in the classroom, in small groups, and for the individual student.

10. Help students determine which graphic organizers work best for their purposes, and encourage them to use graphic organizers collaboratively whenever they can.

11. Help students customize graphic organizers when necessary; e.g., make more or fewer boxes, lines, or blanks, if dictated by the exercise..

OUTLINE

MAIN IDEA: _____

_____

_____

    DETAIL: _____

_____

    DETAIL: _____

_____

    DETAIL: _____

_____

MAIN IDEA: _____

_____

_____

    DETAIL: _____

_____

    DETAIL: _____

_____

    DETAIL: _____

_____

Name _____ Date _____

MAIN IDEA MAP

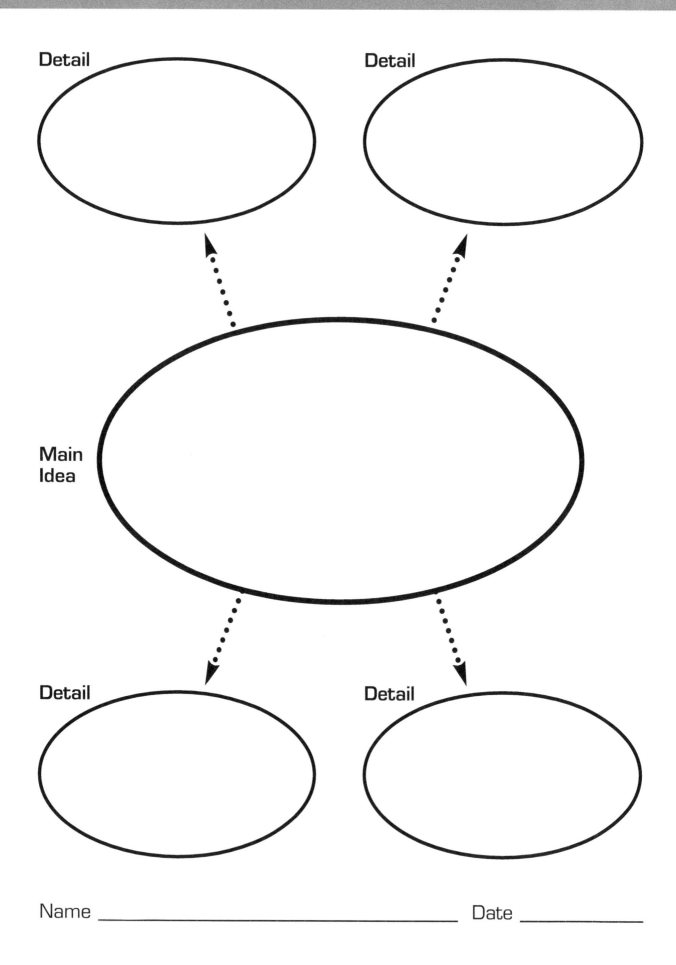

Detail

Detail

Main Idea

Detail

Detail

Name _____ Date _____

K-W-L CHART

K	W	L
What I Know	What I Want to Know	What I Learned

Name _____   Date _____

VENN DIAGRAM

Write differences in the circles. Write similarities where the circles overlap.

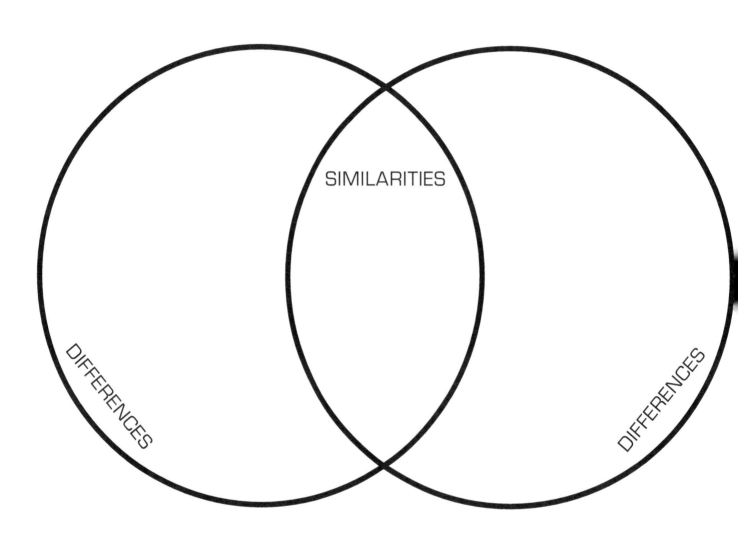

SIMILARITIES

DIFFERENCES

DIFFERENCES

Name _____ Date _____

TIMELINE

DATE

EVENT
Draw lines to connect the event to the correct year on the timeline.

Name _____ Date

SEQUENCE OF EVENTS CHART

Event

Next Event

Next Event

Next Event

Next Event

Name _____ Date _____

T–CHART

Cause | **Effect**

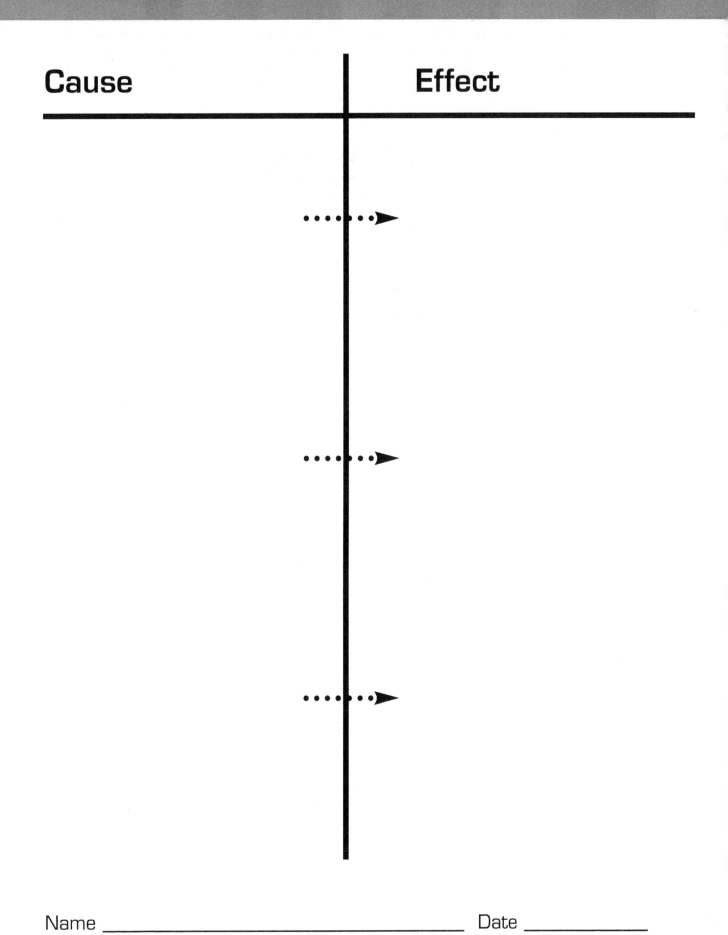

Name _____ Date _____

SCORING RUBRIC

The reproducibles on the following pages have been adapted from this rubric for use as handouts and a student self-scoring activity, with added focus on planning, cooperation, revision and presentation. You may wish to tailor the self-scoring activity—for example, asking students to comment on how low scores could be improved, or focusing only on specific rubric points. Use the Library/Media Center Research Log to help students focus and evaluate their research for projects and assignments.

As with any rubric, you should introduce and explain the rubric before students begin their assignments. The more thoroughly your students understand how they will be evaluated, the better prepared they will be to produce projects that fulfill your expectations.

	ORGANIZATION	CONTENT	ORAL/WRITTEN CONVENTIONS	GROUP PARTICIPATION
4	• Clearly addresses all parts of the writing task. • Demonstrates a clear understanding of purpose and audience. • Maintains a consistent point of view, focus, and organizational structure, including the effective use of transitions. • Includes a clearly presented central idea with relevant facts, details, and/or explanations.	• Demonstrates that the topic was well researched. • Uses only information that was essential and relevant to the topic. • Presents the topic thoroughly and accurately. • Reaches reasonable conclusions clearly based on evidence.	• Contains few, if any, errors in grammar, punctuation, capitalization, or spelling. • Uses a variety of sentence types. • Speaks clearly, using effective volume and intonation.	• Demonstrated high levels of participation and effective decision making. • Planned well and used time efficiently. • Demonstrated ability to negotiate opinions fairly and reach compromise when needed. • Utilized effective visual aids.
3	• Addresses all parts of the writing task. • Demonstrates a general understanding of purpose and audience. • Maintains a mostly consistent point of view, focus, and organizational structure, including the effective use of some transitions. • Presents a central idea with mostly relevant facts, details, and/or explanations.	• Demonstrates that the topic was sufficiently researched. • Uses mainly information that was essential and relevant to the topic. • Presents the topic accurately but leaves some aspects unexplored. • Reaches reasonable conclusions loosely related to evidence.	• Contains some errors in grammar, punctuation, capitalization, or spelling. • Uses a variety of sentence types. • Speaks somewhat clearly, using effective volume and intonation.	• Demonstrated good participation and decision making with few distractions. • Planning and used its time acceptably. • Demonstrated ability to negotiate opinions and compromise with little aggression or unfairness.
2	• Addresses only parts of the writing task. • Demonstrates little understanding of purpose and audience. • Maintains an inconsistent point of view, focus, and/or organizational structure, which may include ineffective or awkward transitions that do not unify important ideas. • Suggests a central idea with limited facts, details, and/or explanations.	• Demonstrates that the topic was minimally researched. • Uses a mix of relevant and irrelevant information. • Presents the topic with some factual errors and leaves some aspects unexplored. • Reaches conclusions that do not stem from evidence presented in the project.	• Contains several errors in grammar, punctuation, capitalization, or spelling. These errors may interfere with the reader's understanding of the writing. • Uses little variety in sentence types. • Speaks unclearly or too quickly. May interfere with the audience's understanding of the project.	• Demonstrated uneven participation or was often off-topic. Task distribution was lopsided. • Did not show a clear plan for the project, and did not use time well. • Allowed one or two opinions to dominate the activity, or had trouble reaching a fair consensus.
1	• Addresses only one part of the writing task. • Demonstrates no understanding of purpose and audience. • Lacks a point of view, focus, organizational structure, and transitions that unify important ideas. • Lacks a central idea but may contain marginally related facts, details, and/or explanations.	• Demonstrates that the topic was poorly researched. • Does not discriminate relevant from irrelevant information. • Presents the topic incompletely, with many factual errors. • Did not reach conclusions.	• Contains serious errors in grammar, punctuation, capitalization, or spelling. These errors interfere with the reader's understanding of the writing. • Uses no sentence variety. • Speaks unclearly. The audience must struggle to understand the project.	• Demonstrated poor participation by the majority of the group. Tasks were completed by a small minority. • Failed to show planning or effective use of time. • Was dominated by a single voice, or allowed hostility to derail the project.

NAME _____   **PROJECT** _____

DATE _____

ORGANIZATION & FOCUS	CONTENT	ORAL/WRITTEN CONVENTIONS	GROUP PARTICIPATION

COMMENTS AND SUGGESTIONS

UNDERSTANDING YOUR SCORE

Organization: Your project should be clear, focused on a main idea, and organized. You should use details and facts to support your main idea.

Content: You should use strong research skills. Your project should be thorough and accurate.

Oral/Written Conventions: For writing projects, you should use good composition, grammar, punctuation, and spelling, with a good variety of sentence types. For oral projects, you should engage the class using good public speaking skills.

Group Participation: Your group should cooperate fairly and use its time well to plan, assign and revise the tasks involved in the project.

NAME _____ **GROUP MEMBERS** _____

_____

_____

_____

Use this worksheet to describe your project by finishing the sentences below.
For individual projects and writing assignments, use the "How I did" section.
For group projects, use both "How I did" and "How we did" sections.

The purpose of this project is to :

Scoring Key =   **4** – extremely well
                         3 – well
                         2 – could have been better
                         1 – not well at all

HOW I DID

I understood the purpose and requirements for this project...

I planned and organized my time and work...

This project showed clear organization that emphasized the central idea...

I supported my point with details and description...

I polished and revised this project...

I utilized correct grammar and good writing/speaking style...

Overall, this project met its purpose...

HOW WE DID

We divided up tasks...

We cooperated and listened to each other...

We talked through what we didn't understand...

We used all our time to make this project the best it could be...

Overall, as a group we worked together...

I contributed and cooperated with the team...

LIBRARY/ MEDIA CENTER RESEARCH LOG

NAME _____

DUE DATE _____

What I Need to **Find**

I need to use:

☐ primary
☐ secondary
sources.

Places I **Know** to Look

Brainstorm: Other Sources and Places to Look

WHAT I FOUND

Rate each source from 1 (low) to 4 (high) in the categories below

helpful   relevant

Title/Author/Location (call # or URL)

	How I Found it						Primary Source	Secondary Source		Book/Periodical	Website	Other
	Suggestion	Library Catalog	Browsing	Internet Search	Web link							

CHAPTER 1

Blackline Master

1. *Nile River:* Its floods provided annual renewal of farmland by dumping rich black dirt along its banks; its water irrigated fields. *Nile Delta:* Marshland forms a natural barrier against enemies. *Cataracts:* These rocky rapids in the Nile protected Egypt against attacks from the south. *Nubia* Traders brought gold to Egypt from Nubia. *Sinai* Turquoise came to Egypt from Sinai.

2. Life along the Nile satisfied people's needs. The floods of the Nile provided farmers with water for irrigation and rich soil for planting; the river was a means of transportation. Beyond the reach of the river was desert.

Chapter Test

A. 1. c 2. a 3. d 4. c 5. d

B. 6. Examples of technology that Egyptian farmers used were irrigation canals and shadufs.

7. Egyptian traders brought back gold from Nubia, turquoise from Sinai, and incense from Punt.

8. In Akhet, the Nile flooded and brought fertile soil. In peret, the floods subsided and farmers planted seeds and irrigated them with water from the Nile. In shemu, the Nile level dropped.

C. Essays should tell about the benefits of being the head of a rich country as well as the king's responsibilities to the gods.

CHAPTER 2

Blackline Master

Front of Palette of Narmer: Falcon (Horus of Nekhen, king's protector); papyrus that falcon is perched on (Lower Egypt); bowling-pin shaped hat on king (White Crown of Upper Egypt); bull's tail (power). *Back of Palette of Narmer:* King's crown (Red crown of Lower Egypt); staff in king's hand (symbol of royalty); entwined panthers (Upper and Lower Egypt, united); bull in bottom scene (power).

Chapter Test

A. 1. a 2. b 3. c 4. d 5. b

B. 6. Egypt 10,000 years ago was wetter and had fields of grass. Elephants and giraffes lived there.

7. The people of Egypt 6,000 years ago herded cattle, planted crops by the Nile, and sometimes lived in small villages.

8. Power was born when one person became the problem solver for everyone.

C. Essays should describe the important symbols on the palette and tell what they stand for.

CHAPTER 3

Blackline Master

The letter should convey the king's awe at having a monument larger than any other before that time and include comments such as the following: the Step Pyramid is different from any other tomb; at 200 feet high within a large complex it shows how great the king is; the false doorways will protect the tomb from robbers; the use of stone means the Step Pyramid will last as a monument to the king's greatness for a long time.

Chapter Test

A. 1. b 2. d 3. a 4. b 5. d

B. 6. It was the first pyramid, the first building constructed out of stone, and the largest building to its time.

7. Working on a pyramid was dangerous because of falling rocks and other accidents.

8. The nilometer readings recorded for those years showed that growing conditions were good.

C. Essays should indicate that Imhotep was not only a good architect but also good at organizing work, handling the king, and caring for the workers.

CHAPTER 4

Blackline Master

Answers will vary.

Chapter Test

A. 1. c 2. b 3. a 4. c 5. d

B. 6. Very few people could read and write in Egypt. Scribes were depended on to record military secrets, magic spells, calculations, payments, births and deaths, and other things.

7. It didn't require hard physical labor.

8. Thomas Young figured out many of the demotic words.

C. Essays should tell how hieroglyphs started as pictures, then developed into symbols that represented things, ideas, and sounds.

CHAPTER 5

Blackline Master

Osiris: He became king of Egypt and married Isis. He was kind. He was killed and chopped into pieces by Seth who was jealous of Osiris. *Isis:* She was married to Osiris. When his murdered body was scattered over Egypt by Seth, Isis found the pieces and with the help of the god, Anubis, put Osiris's body back together. *Seth:* He killed Osiris out of jealousy of Osiris's power and marriage to Isis. Seth represents forces threatening Egypt's *ma'at* (balance and harmony). *Horus:* He was the son of Osiris and Isis. Horus restored *ma'at* to Egypt by killing Seth, his cruel uncle. In battling Seth, Horus was protected by Isis; in the final battle Seth turned himself into a crocodile and Horus speared him.

Chapter Test

A. 1. a 2. b 3. a 4. b 5. c

B. 6. Possible answer: The sun god was the most important god because the sun was there every day and brought life to the world.

7. Life would not be in balance if wars or hunger or lawlessness were occurring.

8. Egyptian priests bathed several times a day, shaved their whole bodies, and pulled their eyelashes out.

C. Essays should tell about how the pharaoh would work with the gods to bring balance to Egypt.

CHAPTER 6

Blackline Master

Step 1—*Ibu*: First the body was washed and then a ceremony with Nile water and natron (salt) was performed. *Reason:* to symbolize rebirth of the person

Step 2—*Per-nefer*: During this step all the organs except the heart were removed from the body. Organs (except for the brain, which is thrown away) are cleaned and stored in jars. The body is stuffed and covered with natron (salt) and left to dry. *Reason:* The dead person's organs are kept so spirits can return to their "home" body. The brain was considered unimportant. Natron helps to dry out the body.

Step 3—*Wabet*: The body is unstuffed and then restuffed with sawdust, rags, natron or even plants. The skin is rubbed with oils and the body is wrapped in linen (500 square yards). A mummy mask is painted and put on top of the mummy's wrapping. *Reason:* The mummy mask helps the person's spirits recognize them after they are wrapped.

Chapter Test

A. 1. b 2. d 3. a 4. d 5. c

B. 6. In the Field of Reeds there was plenty of food; no one had to work; and everyone had perfect health.

7. Anubis had the body of a human and the head of a jackal. His final test was to weigh the dead person's heart against a feather. If the heart was heavier than the feather, the person's heart was fed to the Eater of the Dead, making it impossible for the person's spirit to move on to the Field of Reeds. If heart and feather balanced, the person's spirit was given land in the Field of Reeds.

8. All three texts were meant to help the dead pass the tests to get into the Field of Reeds.

C. Ka had to stay in the tomb with the person's body (or a statue or a painting of the person) or the spirit would die and never reach the Field of Reeds. Ka had to be given food and drink and clothing in the tomb. *Ba* was a living person's personality. Ba looked like a bird with a miniature head of the dead person. After death Ba lived in the tomb but could take any form and go anywhere, even to the land of the living. *Akh* stood for immortality; it shone like a star or the sun, and could live forever in the Field of Reeds.

CHAPTER 7

Blackline Master

1. The king drafted men from villages along the Nile to work on the Great Pyramid and other tombs. The king's representatives traveled to villages and read out the names of those called to serve.

2. The canal connected the Nile to the Mouth of the Lake, a delivery area for barges bringing stones and workers to the pyramid construction site.

3. The giant ovens were used to bake bread for the thousands of construction workers at the site of the Great Pyramid.

4. The sides of the pyramid were covered in limestone blocks weighing 2.5 tons that had to be pushed up a ramp into position by workers.

5. Workers used mud-covered wooden tracks to slide the huge blocks of stone into position.

6. A ramp of stone and rubble was another way workers moved huge blocks of limestone into position on the Great Pyramid.

7. Workers poured water on wooden wedges in the rock walls of the quarry to expand the wood and split the rock into smaller pieces.

8. The Great Pyramid was designed to line up with true north so the king could enter the afterlife.

9. Curses were written on tombs to discourage tomb robbers.

1. 3024 feet (length of each side × 4)

2. about 21 feet per year; about 1.7 feet per month

3. about 281 royal cubits

Chapter Test

A. 1. a 2. c 3. d 4. c 5. b

B. 6. The king's men came to farming villages after the harvests and called off the names of those who would be working on the pyramids.

7. The stone blocks were pushed from the quarry on wooden rails covered with mud and water, were pushed up a ramp on the pyramid, and then lifted into place by ropes and pulleys.where they were lifted into place

8. The orientation had to be just right to help the king get into the Field of Reeds.

C. Essays should retell the myths about the Sphinx described in the chapter.

CHAPTER 8

Blackline Master

Drawings, voice, and narration bubbles should include: Box 1 reasons for Sinuhe's running away; Box 2 how he was treated by nomads; Box 3 why he wanted to return to Egypt; Box 4 what happened when Sinuhe returned to Egypt.

1. The welcome showed that the king did not hold Sinuhe's running away against him. The king knew that Sinuhe would want to see his home again. 2. The moral cited in the chapter is "Egypt is the finest country in the world." Students might also express the moral as: "No matter how comfortable life is in other places, home is best."

Chapter Test

A. 1. c 2. b 3. b 4. a 5. c

B. 6. Egypt was a land of feeble kingdoms because of the civil wars and weak kings.

7. Common Egyptians began to question the old ways; artists and others became more creative.

8. It divides the palace into three areas: the Nursery (living area), Pillared Hall (banquets), and Audience Hall (official business).

C. Essays should show that later writers felt the First Intermediate Period was terrible, but First Intermediate writers tell a different story.

CHAPTER 9

Blackline Master

1. Heat medicinal drugs over hot stones; cover with an upside-down jar with a hole in bottom. To get the benefit of the fumes, breathe through a tube stuck in the jar through hole.

2. Call in a doctor to chant a spell to chase away evil spirits that could be causing the cough.

3. She will study for many years in a "House of Life," reading textbooks to learn symptoms of diseases and treatments for them.

4. If the doctor followed the rules for treating that disease, he or she cannot be punished. If the doctor is tried and found guilty of not following the rules, the punishment is death.

5. A remedy is to eat a combination of crushed hog's tooth inside four sugar cubes for four days.

6. Onion and garlic also work against infections.

7. Yes, some illnesses are beyond a doctor's skill. If a patient has stomach disease, pain in the arms, breast, and one side of the stomach, the doctor will say, "Death threatens."

8. Being able to help people is a *pro*. A *con* is that the punishment for trying an experimental cure is death.

Chapter Test

A. 1. d 2. a 3. b 4. d 5. b

B. 6. Wall paintings of surgery are captioned "Do not let it be painful."

7. Egyptian surgeons performed amputations and tracheotomies and brain surgery, and set broken bones.

8. Honey and garlic were effective in fighting disease because they are antibiotics.

C. Essays should compare similar techniques in diagnosing and treating diseases, and contrast the use of magic in ancient Egypt.

CHAPTER 10

Blackline Master

Hyksos Army—Soldiers: The Hyksos had well-armed professional soldiers. *Weapons:* Hyksos had bows made of horn, sinew, and wood that could shoot arrows farther than wooden bows. *Chariots:* The Hyksos had heavy chariots. *Armor:* The Hyksos wore body armor and leather helmets. *Style of Waging War:* The Hyksos invaded slowly and defended themselves in battles and in the fortress city of Avaris.

Egyptian Army (first battles with Hyksos)—Soldiers: The Egyptians were part-time soldiers. In battles the Egyptians used foreign mercenaries. *Weapons:* Egyptian soldiers had farm tools adapted for battle. *Training:* The Egyptians only trained palace guards and border police, not soldiers. *Armor:* Unknown. *Style of Waging War:* Egyptians scheduled battles; used foreign soldiers so Egyptians did not have to die far from home.

Egyptian Army (at Avaris)—Soldiers: The Egyptian army was now organized, trained, and well equipped. *Weapons:* Egyptian soldiers now used bows and arrows, swords, javelins. *Training:* The Egyptians held battle competitions; shot at targets. *Chariots:* Egyptians had improved on Hyksos chariot: open back so charioteers could jump out and fight; metal axle; driver positioned over axle. *Armor:* Unknown. *Style of Waging War:* Blockaded Avaris, the fortified city of the Hyksos.

Students' responses to the question should include the fact that the many battle successes of the Hyksos made the Egyptians realize the shortcomings of their army and gave them the impetus to make improvements.

Chapter Test

A. 1. c 2. c 3. d 4. a 5. d

B. 6. The Egyptians made the chariots lighter and easier to pull.

7. They had to improve their style of waging war. For instance, they shouldn't have notified their enemy of when they were going to attack.

8. The Egyptians besieged the Hyksos at Avaris. The two sides then concluded a treaty by which the Hyksos left Egypt.

C. Essays should explain that the Egyptians didn't like foreigners controlling their land.

CHAPTER 11

Blackline Master

Hatshepsut—Leadership: She chose to rule as a king and convinced Egyptians that she was divine and that the gods recognized her as king. *Relations with Other Powers:* Expanded Egypt's contact and trade with Punt, a faraway African land. *Contributions to Egypt:* Added to Egypt's wealth through explorations and trade; especially by sending an expedition to Punt.

Thutmose III—Leadership: He was a warrior king who had trained in the army and was a general before he became king. He made a bold move against the rebels at Megiddo. *Relations with Other Powers:* When rebels took the important trading city of Megiddo (in present-day Israel), Thutmose III attacked and carried out a seven-month siege. Showed the world that Egypt would flourish under a warrior king. *Contributions to Egypt:* Under his rule Egypt experienced a golden age and expanded its territory.

Chapter Test

A. 1. b 2. c 3. b 4. d 5. a

B. 6. The trade expedition brought back ebony, incense, ivory, cosmetics, animals and animal skins.

7. Megiddo had been taken over by rebels, and Thutmose III had to reassert Egypt's power there.

8. He decided to take the difficult route straight to the city. The rebels were not expecting this and were taken by surprise.

C. Students' essays about the pharaohs' contributions will vary, but should be supported by details from the chapter.

CHAPTER 12

Blackline Master

1. In the story, the shipwrecked sailor offers to repay the serpent's kindness with things Egyptians valued highly—sacred oils, perfumes, and incense. The sailor receives gifts from the serpent that show what Egyptians considered valuable: precious perfumes, sweet woods, kohl, and animals and animal products such as baboons, apes, ivory tusks.

2. The serpent's appearance and speech (identifying himself as a prince) shows that the isle is magical. Egyptians thought of Punt the same way.

3. *Mining:* The ship the sailor was on was headed for the pharaoh's mines. *travel by sea* The sailor was traveling by ship. *Power of serpents:* The serpent, who says he is a prince of Punt, is covered in symbols of wealth and power—a beard (such as kings wore), gold, and lazuli. He has the power to foretell the future and to save the sailor and can afford to give him precious gifts. *Mysteries of Punt:* Like Punt, the island is mysterious (it will be changed into waves, it is ruled by a serpent). *Pride in Egypt:* The Egyptian sailors on the shipwrecked sailor's ship are described as having "hearts stronger than lions." The sailor promises to send the serpent valuable gifts from Egypt. *Loyalty to a ruler:* The shipwrecked sailor says "I bowed myself before him," showing loyalty to the serpent ruler.

Chapter Test

A. 1. c 2. b 3. c 4. d 5. c

B. 6. Egyptians believed jewelry could protect against drowning and one's enemies.

7. Since fleas were a problem, Egyptians shaved off their own hair and wore wigs to look fashionable.

8. It was not correct to wear clothing made of animal skins in front of gods who were thought to be part animal.

C. Students' essays will vary, but should show an understanding of Egyptian style.

CHAPTER 13

Blackline Master

Overseer of Works—As Overseer of Works the vizier was in charge of all the king's engineering projects, such as building monuments, tombs, and temples or digging and maintaining waterways. He made sure that men and materials were provided where they were needed. *Keeper of the Seal*—As Keeper of the Seal the vizier was responsible for keeping the records of all marriage contracts, wills, deeds to property, court transcripts and counts of people and cattle. He was in charge of taxes and the records of the Nile's rise and fall. *Overseer of Justice*—The vizier was responsible for law and order which involved capturing, sometimes torturing, and then punishing criminals.

The title "Eyes and Ears of the Sovereign" is a good description of a vizier because to keep the kingdom running smoothly the vizier had to know what was going on. People under the vizier reported to him what they saw (eyes) and heard (ears) so he could order the necessary action if he decided there was a threat to law and order.

Chapter Test

A. 1. c 2. b 3. b 4. c 5. b

B. 6. Egyptians did not use imprisonment for punishment, so they would not need so many prisons.

7. Punishments became more severe because the middle class was growing larger and demanded such punishment.

8. Any citizen, whether royal or not, could become vizier.

C. The vizier's "hats" included responsibility for law and order; engineering projects, such as tombs and temples and waterways; and records, such as wills, head counts of people and cattle, marriage contracts, deeds, and the Nile's rise and fall. The vizier could not do all this alone so many people reported to him. However, the person ultimately responsible for keeping the kingdom running smoothly was the vizier.

CHAPTER 14

Blackline Master

1. Amarna-Hattusa: almost 900 miles; Amarna-Babylon: almost 900 miles; Amarna-Troy: about 950 miles

2. The city that is farthest east on the map is Babylon. The city that is farthest west is Mycenae.

3. Knossos on Crete communicated with Amarna. It is about 650 miles away.

4. Ugarit is in Mittani. The king of Mittani wrote to Queen Tiy to complain about getting gold-plated statues instead of massive gold ones.

Chapter Test

A. 1. b 2. b 3. c 4. d 5. b

B. 6. Rulers of other countries are constantly asking for money or for help.

7. The letters tell which countries Egypt dominated and which were its equals.

8. The vassals either broke away from Egyptian control or were conquered by other kingdoms.

C. Essays should trace the route the Amarna Letters took to the British Museum, and state that there are now rules against taking artifacts that way.

CHAPTER 15

Blackline Master

1. It was in an isolated spot with limestone cliffs and "windswept desert."

2. Akhenaten's goal was to change the way Egyptians worshipped; his new capital city dedicated to the sun god symbolized a new beginning.

3. The site was on the Nile River, good for transportation; limestone used for building the new city was found nearby.

4. Akhenaten paid attention only to Amarna, a city dedicated to the sun god. Egyptians in other parts of the country resented paying taxes to support a single city at the expense of the rest of the country.

5. The North Palace: between 2 and 3 miles; the Great Temple: a little over a mile; the Great Palace: a little over a mile.

6. The Great Temple at Amarna was dedicated to one god, not many. It was open to the sun, not dark and gloomy like older temples.

Chapter Test

A. 1. b 2. b 3. c 4. c 5. d

B. 6. He built Amarna along the Nile between Memphis and Thebes.

7. The new temple was open and well lit, whereas the older temples were enclosed and dark.

8. Akhenaten built a university to train the new priests for his religion.

C. Essays should indicate that Akhenaten's devotion to Aten (and Amarna) took the pharaoh's attention away from other parts of Egypt and from Egypt's foreign subjects.

CHAPTER 16

Blackline Master

1. H 2. F 3. B 4. D 5. J 6. E 7. C 8. A 9. G 10. I

Students' agreement or disagreement with the statement should be supported with details from the chapter.

Chapter Test

A. 1. a 2. b 3. a 4. c 5. b

B. 6. Everything was photographed in case the articles disintegrated when they were touched.

7. All of the articles had to be photographed and have its details and placement recorded.

8. Modern scientists could have told what month Tut was buried, how he died, the condition of his spine, his DNA, and how his face looked.

C. Essays should tell about the challenges of reinvigorating Egypt after the neglectful reign of Akhenaten.

CHAPTER 17

Blackline Master

Pets: Most children had pets that included not only cats and dogs but ferrets, geese, monkeys, and falcons. *Toys:* Even poor children had toys. Some were mechanical, with jaws that opened and shut and tails that wagged. There were dolls with real hair, clothes and furniture and tops, balls, boats, and board games. *Education:* Most children never learned to read and write. Privileged children, usually boys, were taught starting at age five. They might go to a House of Instruction to learn skills for future jobs, or have a tutor come to their home. Education meant memorizing and reciting passages from texts or writing them over and over again. *Protection from disease:* Children were breast-fed until age three which protected them from parasites. Parents tied amulets around children's necks and recited spells to keep them healthy and safe. An amulet might contain a written spell to protect the child. Sometimes charms for specific protections (an ibis for healing) were hung from a necklace around a child's neck. Students' paragraphs will vary but should be supported with details from the chapter.

Chapter Test

A. 1. c 2. c 3. c 4. c 5. a

B. 6. Nakht was not mummified, so all of his body parts can be studied.

7. Nakht was always short of breath because he suffered from black lung disease and desert lung disease.

8. Most Egyptian children played with toys and enjoyed games and pets.

C. Essays should include details about toys, pets, and play as well as the age at which ancient Egyptians married.

CHAPTER 18

Blackline Master

Scene 1: D Scene 2: A Scene 3: B

Students' paragraphs should explain that Ramesses claimed that he alone was responsible for the victory over the Hittites and that he did not mention his soldiers who arrived to save the day.

Chapter Test

A. 1. b 2. d 3. a 4. b 5. d

B. 6. The Hittites had increased their control in Syria during the reign of Akhenaten, and Ramesses wanted to take back that control.

7. The Hittites didn't capture Ramesses because they stopped to loot the Egyptian camp.

8. The battled ended in a draw, and then the two kingdoms decided to sign a treaty.

C. Essays should contrast Ramesses's positive qualities with his negative ones, and evaluate whether he was "great."

CHAPTER 19

Blackline Master

Column 1: entrance hall, room for receiving guests (B, G, H), kitchen (A, C, D, E), roof (F)

Column 3: griddle stones used for cooking; *woven mat* for seating family or guests; *wood for fire* used for cooking; *onions* part of a meal, also used as medicine; *oven* used to make bread, made kitchen area very hot; *beds* were taken to the roof where it was cooler; *folding stools* used for seating guests; *statues of gods* protected home.

Students' diary entries might mention the village was home to skilled craftsmen who build tombs in the Valley of the Kings. "Likes" might be the close-knit community and houses that could be built or rebuilt easily. "Dislikes" might include crowded conditions, heat, smells, fleas, and lice.

Chapter Test

A. 1. b 2. d 3. a 4. b 5. a

B. 6. The residents used the ruins of the previous home as the foundations for their new home.

7. The typical house had an entrance hall, a main living room, and a kitchen in the back. People often ate and slept on the roof.

8. To keep fleas and pests away, the residents would cover their doorways with a cloth flap, sprinkle the house with natron, place the fat of cat on things, and place an onion by a snake hole.

C. Students' essays will vary.

CHAPTER 20

Blackline Master

Red Arrows (showing Sea Peoples' advance): by land from northeast to southern Palestine (eastern shore of Mediterranean Sea) and by sea from northeast to Nile Delta; *Green Arrows* (Egyptian defense)—from Egypt toward the advance of Sea Peoples in southern Palestine and toward Nile Delta; *Red and Green Boats:* in Nile Delta to show position of naval battle. Students' paragraphs should show they understand (1) that the Egyptians won the battle at the mouth of the Nile because their ships used oars and could maneuver better than the Sea Peoples' sailing ships and (2) that because of Egyptians' deep-seated fear of the "Great Green" (Mediterranean Sea) and the Sea Peoples' superior sea-going ships the Sea Peoples would probably have won a sea battle.

Chapter Test

A. 1. a 2. d 3. b 4. a 5. c

B. 6. He didn't want to take the chance of losing in Egypt and being overrun by the Sea Peoples.

7. The Sea Peoples, who were better on the open water, might have beaten the Egyptians, who were not skilled sailors.

8. The Egyptian navy trapped the Sea Peoples' boats in the narrow river mouths of the Nile and maneuvered them close to shore, where the Egyptian archers could shoot at them.

C. Essays should show that *ma'at* means balance and that the Sea Peoples invasion meant chaos. By defeating the Sea Peoples, Ramesses restored peace and balance in Egyptian life.

CHAPTER 21

Blackline Master

Students' scripts for each scene should retell the story of Rhodopis told in this chapter.

Chapter Test

A. 1. d 2. c 3. a 4. c 5. a

B. 6. Answers will vary.

7. It was called the "sacred ratio" because the proportion repeats throughout the natural world.

8. The main character liked music because everyone in Egypt liked music.

C. Essays should include these characteristics: obedience to rules; use of frontalism, use of magic images (such as a spear in a crocodile), and the use of the "sacred ratio"

CHAPTER 22

Blackline Master

1. C; Led to anger against Kushite rule in Upper Egypt.
2. F; Rebellion aroused King Piye to act to preserve Egypt and put down rebellion.
3. A; Piye's intervention was not an invasion, but a rescue of Egypt.
4. B Armies clashed on land and water; Kushite soldiers crushed Egyptians.
5. D; Showed that Piye thought of Kush as home.
6. E; Shows that Piye was a compassionate man with Egypt's best interests at heart.

Chapter Test

A. 1. b 2. a 3. a 4. b 5. d
B. 6. Egypt had split into two weak lands.
7. Egypt was fated to be ruled by foreigners.
8. Religion had such a strong influence on life that even a conqueror had to observe its rituals.
C. Essays should explain that when the Egyptians organized a rebellion against Kushite rule, King Piye brought his army into Egypt. Once Egypt was reunited, King Piye returned to Kush to rule from there.

CHAPTER 23

Blackline Master

Students' plans of their cities will vary but should be logical and consistent. Students' responses to questions about their cities should be appropriate and thoughtful.

Chapter Test

A. 1. b 2. b 3. a 4. c 5. b
B. 6. He had defeated the Persians, who had taxed the Egyptians heavily and didn't respect their gods and traditions.
7. Pharos was on the Mediterranean shore and had a protected harbor.
8. When their water ran out, a storm refilled their containers. When they were lost in the desert, two black ravens came to guide them. When Alexander reached Siwah, the priest said "Oh, son of god."
C. Students' essays will vary, but their opinions should be supported with details from the chapter.

CHAPTER 24

Blackline Master

1. Students should place the CE dates above the line where the years BCE and 1 CE are shown; BCE dates below the line.
2. 21st CE, 2000 CE; 2nd BCE, 100 BCE; 16th BCE, 1500 BCE; 6th CE, 500 CE; 21st BCE, 2000 BCE
3. 2500 CE; 2500 BCE

Chapter Test

A. 1. d 2. a 3. b 4. c 5. b
B. 6. Agents bought up other libraries. Books were copied. Books were confiscated from boats that docked in the harbor, the originals were kept and copies were returned.
7. Ptolemy promised Rome a year's worth of grain if they would use their military to keep him on his throne.
8. Ptolemy the geographer studied the movements of heavenly bodies and used longitude and latitude to make accurate maps.
C. Essays should note that maps, math, astronomy, and a system for organizing books in the school library can all be traced back to scholars who taught and studied in Alexandria.

WRAP-UP TEST

1. Students should indicate that the Nile flows north into the Mediterranean Sea; and the mouth of the Nile should show the branching waterways of the delta. Answers will vary, but should include the following information: the annual flooding of the Nile deposited rich earth on farmer's fields. The rising floodwaters were measured by a nilometer and compared to the floods of previous years. Farmers used a *shaduf*, a weighted bucket, to scoop water out of the river to irrigate their fields.

2. Bes, the household god, comforted women during childbirth; the pharaoh was a god and was his people's connection to the gods; the god who controlled flooding was responsible for the well-being of Egypt; in order to reach the afterlife, people had to pass tests set by the gods.

3. Students' paragraphs should indicate the pyramid was the tomb of Khufu (Cheops) and was his pathway to the afterlife; workers were often drafted by the king to work on the pyramid; challenges included cutting and moving heavy blocks of limestone from a quarry to the pyramid and then into position on the pyramid.

4. Kush is located south of Egypt. Students' paragraphs should note that Kush provided gold to Egypt and that King Piye of Kush took responsibility for uniting Upper and Lower Egypt and restoring the power and influence of Egypt during the Third Intermediate Period.

5. *Who:* Viziers were men (in some cases women) who were the pharaoh's second-in-command. Viziers came from different levels of society and could serve under more than one pharaoh. *What:* The vizier's three main responsibilities were keeping the records (such as marriage contracts, head counts, property deeds), directing engineering projects and supplying men and materials; and keeping law and order. *Why:* The vizier's power came from being the "eyes and ears" of the pharaoh. He had to know what was going on in order to do his job; he had to have power to make things happen.

6. *Rosetta Stone:* Made it possible to figure out hieroglyphics and read Egyptian texts in the original. *Tomb of Tutankhamen:* Showed the level of luxury in which pharaohs lived; shed light on mummifying practices, and the death of Tutankhamen. *Ostraca at Deir el-Medina:* The notes on ostraca show the daily concerns of village life: employment, barter, human relations. *Amarna Letters:* Give insights into diplomacy during Amenhotep III's reign; most of the letters concern grievances and desires of the letter-writers.

7. 1C, 2, 3D, 4B. *Sinuhe* reminded generations of Egyptians that Egypt was the best country in the world. *Shipwrecked Sailor* reveals beliefs about Punt, a magical land full of valuable goods. *Wenamun* showed how Egypt's power had faded. *Rhodopis* reveals the universality of the Cinderella story.

8. Students' first paragraphs should describe frontalism and explain why kings and important people are shown larger than people around them. In the second paragraph students should present the theory that artists in the Amarna period drew people more realistically.

9. *Hyksos* brought to Egypt hump-backed cattle, apples, olives, an improved loom and potters' wheel but were still an irritant to Egyptians. After early battles, the Egyptian army adapted the Hyksos chariot and improved it; the army also began training seriously and in the end forced the Hyksos to leave. *Hittites* challenged Egypt's power by taking over Qadesh; after Ramesses II led Egyptian army against the Hittites at Qadesh, the countries signed the first known mutual assistance treaty. *Sea Peoples* caused Ramesses III to build up defenses in the Nile delta and prepare to resist invasion. The Egyptians defeated the Sea Peoples when their warships met in the narrow channels of the Nile Delta.

10. 1. H 2. C 3. B 4. F 5. H 6. I 7. A 8. J 9. G 10. D. Students' choices will vary, but their ideas should be supported with details from the book.

ANSWERS FOR THE STUDENT STUDY GUIDE

CHAPTER 1

With a Parent or Partner   Sentences should be about measuring devices such as triple balance beams, laser devices, tape measures, and digital thermometers.

Cast of Characters

Pharaoh Pepi II: *young, interested, commanding*
Harkhuf: *proud, respectful*

Word Bank   gauge; caravans; barren; sacrifices; rapids; Students should write a sentence using *anguish*.

All Over the Map   Ask students to show work.

Working with Primary Sources   Students' journal entries will vary.

CHAPTER 2

Cast of Characters

Narmer is celebrated as the first king to unite Upper and Lower Egypt. Some think Menes is the king who united Upper and Lower Egypt, although some say Menes was the same person as Narmer.

Word Bank   chaos; legend; conquered; harmony; Students should write a sentence using *palette* and *pigments*.

All Over the Map   Ask students to show their work. 1. Egypt was once called the "two lands" because it was separated into Upper and Lower Egypt. 2. The Nile flows northward. 3. Gravity causes the Nile to flow from high land (Upper Egypt) to low land (Lower Egypt). 4. Upper Egypt is where the highlands are. Lower Egypt is near sea level at the Mediterranean.

Working with Primary Sources   The Palette of Narmer is like a comic book because it tells a story in pictures, words, and symbols. Review students' own comic books.

CHAPTER 3

Cast of Characters

Djoser: Powerful king who built the first pyramid as his tomb
Manetho: Egyptian historian put the reigns of the Egyptian kings in order
Imhotep: Architect and scientist who designed Djoser's pyramid
Edwin Smith: Egyptologist who bought a papyrus said to be a copy of a medical document written by Imhotep

What Happened When?

2700 BCE: Old Kingdom Period; Egyptians were irrigating more and more land for farming.
1862 CE: Edwin Smith buys papyrus that is thought to be copy of medical document written by Imhotep in the 30th century BCE.
4,562 years passed between these two events.

Word Bank   1. masons 2. inundation 3. architect 4. granaries
Students should write a sentence using *artisan*.

Critical Thinking   1. fact 2. opinion 3. fact 4. fact 5. opinion 6. fact 7. opinion 8. fact

Working with Primary Sources   1. Building the pyramids was dangerous because of the chance of being struck and injured and killed by dropped objects. 2. Imhotep probably discovered his medical treatments and cures from trial and error and more ancient authorities.

Write About It   Students' paragraphs will vary but should be based on the information in the chapter.

CHAPTER 4

Cast of Characters

Bekenkhons: Scribe who spent 11 years as an apprentice
Ptolemy V: Pharaoh to whom Rosetta Stone was addressed
Napoleon: French leader whose soldiers dug up the Rosetta Stone in 1799 CE
Thomas Young: English scholar who first translated some of the Rosetta Stone

What Happened When?

About 3100 BCE: Some of the earliest Egyptian writing.
196 BCE: Date text on Rosetta Stone was composed.
1799 CE: Rosetta Stone found by French troops.
The year 196 BCE came after the year 3100 BCE.

Word Bank   hieroglyphics; demotics; democracy

Sequence of Events   Peel the skin off the papyrus stem. Slice the stem into thin strips. Lay the strips together, slightly overlapping. Cover the reed strips with linen, then pound the sheet with a mallet. The crushed reeds ooze sticky sap. The dried sap will glue the strips together. Arrange another layer on top, going in the opposite direction. Glue the sheets together with flour and water paste.

Working with Primary Sources   Students' "report cards" for Bekenkhons will vary.

CHAPTER 5

Cast of Characters

Neferhotep: pharaoh who took special care to follow the rituals at the temple at Abydos
Plutarch: Greek historian who gave the most complete version of the Great Hymn to Osiris
David O'Connor: archaeologist who is excavating Abydos
William Petrie: one of the first excavators of Abydos

What Happened When?

1741–1730 BCE: King Neferhotep ruled Egypt.
1st century CE: Plutarch wrote down the *Great Hymn of Osiris*.
1967 CE: David O'Connor started excavating at Abydos in this year.

Word Bank   scarab; stela; shrines; archaeologist
Students' sentences should include *sacred* and *excavate*.

Comprehension   Balance was important to Egyptians, since it mean that the gods were happy and that their lives would be good.

Working with Primary Sources   1. Egypt is a good place to learn about early cultures because its archaeology, in terms of monuments, art, and objects of daily life, have survived much better than in other places. 2. Winter and spring are good time to excavate because they are the cooler seasons. 3. Snakes and scorpions present dangers to archaeologists in Egypt. 4. Recording exactly where artifacts are found helps in understanding how the objects were used. 5. Botanists can tell where a certain type of wood came from.

CHAPTER 6

Cast of Characters

Herodotus: Greek historian who wrote about mummification in the 5th century BCE
Diodorus Siculus: Greek historian who wrote about mummification in the 1st century BCE

Comprehension   1. Herodotus and Diodorus Siculus were from Greece. 2. Diodorus Siculus wrote 40 books of world history. 3. Herodotus is known as the "father of history."

What Happened When?

about 2375–2184 BCE: The Pyramid Texts were written.
about 1500–250 BCE: The Book of the Dead was written.

Critical Thinking   1. The spirits correctly answered the questions of the gatekeepers. SO The gatekeepers allowed them through the labyrinth. 2. The spirits successfully declared their innocence before 42 gods. SO The spirits moved on to the final test. 3. The dead person's heart balanced with truthfulness and justice. SO The deceased was given a plot in the Field of Reeds. 4. The dead person's heart weighed heavy with sin. SO The spirits spent eternity haunting the living.

Working with Primary Sources   Old Kingdom: only pharaohs allowed into Field of Reeds, Pyramid Texts, kings had answers and spells buried with them.   Middle Kingdom: Field of Reeds open to all, Coffin Texts, spells written on sides of coffins.   New Kingdom: spells written on scrolls, Book of the Dead, scrolls buried with the body.   All: kings had to answer questions.

Write About It   1. The Egyptians thought the heart was the most important bodily organ. 2. It might take two weeks to wrap a body in linen. 3. The painted mask helped Ka and Ba recognize their body. 4. Natron (salt from the Nile) was the kind of salt used to dry out the body.

CHAPTER 7

Cast of Characters

Khufu: pharaoh who built the Great Pyramid at Giza
Thutmose IV: This king is an important character in the legend of the Sphinx

What Happened When?

The Dream Stela, which sits between the Sphinx's paws, was carved about 1419–1386 BCE.

Word Bank   1. mennefer 2. mer

Do the Math   1. 2,000 pounds equals 1 ton 2. A 40-ton stone block would weigh 80,000 pounds.

Sequence of Events   Steps to move the stone blocks into place: Push blocks on mud-covered wooden tracks to pyramid. Push blocks up stone-and-rubble ramp. Lift stones into place with rope and pulleys.

Working with Primary Sources   1. The Sphinx was protected from crumbling because it was mostly buried in sand. 2. The Dream Stela describes the legend of how Thutmose IV became king. 3. If Prince Thutmose would clear away the sand, the Sphinx would make him king. 4. Thutmose may have made up the story to cover his murder of his brother.

CHAPTER 8

Cast of Characters

Pepi II: aging king who lost power to the governors
Ankhtyfy: Egyptian governor during the First Intermediate Period who bragged about his powers
Sinuhe: royal guard about whose life a popular tale was written
Amenemhet: king who reunited Egypt in the First Intermediate Period but was murdered
Senwosert: the son of Amenemhet

What Happened When?

2278 BCE: The reign of Pepi II began.
1991–1926 BCE: The Tale of Sinuhe was written.

Timeline   Events on students' timelines should be in this order: Pepi II's reign; end of Pepi II's reign; vertical loom invented; Ankhtyfy governed two provinces; return of centralized power.

Word Bank   anarchy; monarchy; intermediate   Students' lists of words with the prefix *inter-* will vary.

Critical Thinking   Positive: people began to think for themselves, others besides the king might enter the afterlife, artists painted in new styles, artisans no longer told how things must be done, inventions such as the vertical loom. Negative: "festering from civil wars," "bathed in blood," "mercy has perished."

Working with Primary Sources   Sinuhe fled Egypt because he was scared that he would also be killed. Students' outlines of the Tale of Sinuhe will vary but should include the main ideas and details described in the chapter.

CHAPTER 9

Cast of Characters

Homer: Greek poet who wrote about Egyptian doctors around 750 BCE
Diodorus Siculus: Greek historian who wrote about the ancient laws of Egyptian doctors
Herodotus: Greek historian who wrote about specialization amongst Egyptian doctors

What Happened When?

about 1600 BCE: The Edwin Smith Papyrus was written.
about 1550 BCE: The Ebers Papyrus was written.
about 750 BCE: Homer wrote about Egyptian doctors in The Odyssey.

Word Bank   1. peru-ankh   2. obsidian

Critical Thinking

Egyptian Medicine: evil spirits cause illness, excrement used as medicine, obsidian instruments used. *Modern Medicine:* vaccines, man-made antibiotics used. *Both:* doctors study many years, medical textbooks studied, doctors specialize, herbal medicines used, pulse checked, surgery performed, broken bones set, amputations performed, anesthesia given, medication dosages adjusted.

Write About It

asthma: Use an inhaler made of stones and a reed tube. *cough:* Chant a spell to drive out evil spirits. *cold:* Take a dose of milk from a mother with a boy baby and a magic chant. *indigestion:* Eat a crushed hog's tooth and four sugar cakes for four days. *cut:* Mix scribe's excrement with milk and apply as poultice. *heart attack:* No cure—"death threatens." Students' letters to friends will vary but should include details from the chapter.

CHAPTER 10

Cast of Characters

Manetho: Egyptian historian who divided Egypt's pharaohs into dynasties
Seqenenre: king of Egypt who was killed in battle with Hyksos
Ahmose: Egyptian soldier whose battles with Hyksos were recorded in tomb inscription
Ahhotep: Queen of Egypt who fought against Hyksos
Josephus Flavius: Roman historian who wrote about Egyptian battles against Hyksos

What Happened When?

about 1574–1550 BCE: War between Egyptians and Hyksos.
about 1550 BCE: Final siege of the town of Avaris.
about 1212–1202 BCE: Papyrus Sallier I, about King Seqenenre, is written.
about 300 BCE: Manetho writes Aegyptiaca.

Timeline In order, the periods are Early Dynastic Period (3050–2686 BCE), Old Kingdom Period (2686–2184 BCE), First Intermediate Period (2181–2040 BCE), Middle Kingdom Period (2040–1782 BCE), and Second Intermediate Period (1782–1570 BCE).

Word Bank heqa-khasut; chiefs of foreign lands

Comprehension 1. Queen Ahhotep I lived to be 90 years old. 2. It was not typical for someone to live that long. 3. Students' answers and sources will vary.

Critical Thinking King Seqenenre was insulted by the Hyksos king's complaints about the royal hippos. SO Egypt went to war with the Hyksos. Egyptians did not want to fight and die away from home. SO The king hired foreign mercenaries to fight battles outside of Egypt. The Egyptians were farmers and the Hyksos were professional soldiers with body armor, leather helmets, and powerful bows. SO The Hyksos won the first battles with the Egyptians. The Egyptians trained to improve their skills. SO The Egyptians became an organized military power.

All Over the Map Compare students' maps against map on page 76.

CHAPTER 11

Cast of Characters

Hatshepsut: Female king of Egypt who ruled for her son
Thutmose II: Husband of Hatshepsut and father of Thutmose III
Thutmose III: Son of Hatshepshut, who fought rebels at Megiddo, the first recorded battle in history

What Happened When?

1504 BCE: Queen Hatshepsut becomes king of Egypt.
1483 BCE: Thutmose III becomes king.

Word Bank divine; mortal Students' sentences should include *destiny*.

Sequence of Events Order of sentences: Five sailing ships leave Egypt. Small boats are loaded with items to trade. Egyptian traders come to a village in Punt. Traders meet village chief. Traders give villagers gifts. Villagers show Egyptian traders where to find ebony and incense. Sailors unload riches from Punt. Besides ebony and incense, the traders brought back fragrant woods, ivory, eye-cosmetics, animals of different kinds, and trees. The phrase "as her due" means that Hatshepsut accepted all of the items from Punt because they belonged to her as pharaoh.

Working with Primary Sources Students' outlines will vary but should include the main ideas and details about Thutmose III from the chapter.

CHAPTER 12

Cast of Characters

Herodotus: Greek historian who wrote about ancient Egypt
Hatshepsut wore a fake beard because she was a woman and couldn't grow a real one.

What Happened When?

about 2345–2181 BCE: time period of 6th Dynasty
about 2000 BCE: *The Tale of a Shipwrecked Sailor* written.
about 1550 BCE: Ebers Papyrus written.

Word Bank barbarian; linen; flax; fragrances; alabaster Students' sentences should include *rituals*.

Critical Thinking Do: wear gold or silver jewelry, wear a palm frond wig, tie a scented wax cone on top of your head, wear eye makeup, put chopped lettuce on your bald spot, shave your beard. *Don't:* wear your hair long, wear your sandals outdoors, wear leather.

Working with Primary Sources Students' essays and designs will vary but should show evidence of understanding the details in the chapter.

CHAPTER 13

Cast of Characters

Amenhotep III: *strong, diplomat, magnificent*
Tiy: *beautiful*
Students' sentences will vary.

What Happened When?

Scarab 1: Year 2—Marriage Scarab.
Scarab 2: Year 2—Big Game Hunting.
Scarab 3: Year 10: Arrival of Foreign Princess to Join Harem.
Scarab 4: Year 11—Lake for Queen Tiy.
Amenhotep III would have been about 17 years old in Year 5 of his reign.

Word Bank harem; vizier; illiterate; amputation Students' sentences should include *elite*.

Critical Thinking tax evasion: 100 blows *stealing cattle:* amputation of nose and ears *perjury:* death Other forms of punishment were assignment to labor gangs, work in the quarries, execution and destruction of the body

Working with Primary Sources Perjury means "lying while under an oath to tell the truth." Students' paragraphs will vary.

Comprehension Vizier's duties: keep law and order; in charge of taxes, records, troop movement, tracking the rise and fall of the Nile; takes reports from governors; Overseer of Works; Keeper of the Seal.

CHAPTER 14

Cast of Characters

E. A. Wallis Budge: representative of British Museum who got some of the Amarna Letters
Monsieur Grebaut: Egyptian official in charge of antiquities
Nimmuriya: another name of Amenhotep III
Tiy: Amenhotep III's wife

What Happened When?

1386–1334 BCE: Amarna Letters are written.
1887 CE: First Amarna Letters are found by an Egyptian peasant woman.
1894–1924 CE: E. A. Wallis Budge is Curator of Egyptian Antiquities at the British Museum.

Word Bank diplomacy; dominion; alliance; curator Students' sentences should include *antiquities* and *steamer*.

Sequence of Events Events in their proper order: The British Museum sent Budge to Egypt to find the tablets discovered in Amarna. Monsieur Grebaut had Budge followed in Egypt. The steamer captain and the villagers delayed Monsieur Grebaut's delivery of an arrest warrant to Budge. Budge discovered that the Amarna tablets were diplomatic letters. Budge managed to take some of the Amarna Letters back to England.

All Over the Map Check students' maps against map on page 105.

CHAPTER 15

Cast of Characters

Akhenaten: Egyptian king who tried to start new religion
Nefertiti: wife of Akhenaten

What Happened When?

1350–1334 BCE: Reign of Amenhotep IV (Akhenaten)
750 BCE: In the *Iliad*, Homer calls Thebes "Hundred-Gated Thebes." The mid-1300s BCE were a golden age for Egypt because it was extremely rich, gifts came in from nations seeking alliances from all over the known world, huge temples and other buildings were being built.

Word Bank embalmers; monotheist, proverb Students' lists of words with the prefix *mono-* will vary.

Critical Thinking

Memphis: scribes, business, government, documents, northern capital, archives, governors Thebes: temples, priests, columns, logs, southern capital, Amen, secret rituals

Comprehension

A *heretic* is someone who disagrees with the accepted religion. Students' paragraphs should note how Akhenaten disagreed with accepted Egyptian religion.

Working with Primary Sources

Students should recognize that the proverb means that you shouldn't pass along gossip that you have heard, and that seeing something with your own eyes is more trustworthy than hearing about it from someone else. Students' paragraphs will vary.

CHAPTER 16

Cast of Characters

Howard Carter: excavator of the tomb of Tutankhamen
Tutankhamen: Young king of Egypt after Akhenaten
Maya: Tutankhamen's treasurer
Ay: king who followed Tutankhamen
Horemheb: Tutankhamen's general; king who followed Ay

What Happened When?

November 5: Carter uncovers steps to tomb of unknown person.
November 24: Workmen finish clearing the stairway. Tomb is revealed to be Tutaknhamen's.
November 26: Carter uncovers antechamber filled with burial objects.
November 27: Carter finds Tutankhamen's burial place.

Word Bank sarcophagus Botany could tell things about flowers or plants found in the tomb. Radiology could scan the mummy and tell things about it without damaging it.

Critical Thinking

Students' outlines will vary, but should include main ideas and details from the chapter.

Comprehension

1. Tutankhamen was ten when he became king.
2. Tutankhamen was 19 when he died. 3. He was about five feet six inches tall and thin. 4. He changed his name so he wouldn't be associated with Akhenaten. 5. It was heavy because it was solid gold. 6. His body had stuck to his coffin because priests had poured sacred oils over the mummy and coffin. 7. We can use computers to recreate faces. 8. The cobra and the vulture symbolize Upper and Lower Egypt. They were on the likeness of Tutankhamen because he was ruler of both lands.

CHAPTER 17

Word Bank ibis; amulets; apprentice Students' sentences should use *spell*. Possible examples of onomatopoeia: 1. drip 2. swish 3. vroom 4. bowwow 5. honk 6. ding dong 7. boom

Comprehension

1. The body of Nakht is so valuable to us because it wasn't mummified, and so we can learn things about the health of young people in ancient Egypt. 2. Nakht suffered from black lung disease, desert lung disease, malaria, and parasites that caused damage to organs, nausea, diarrhea, vomiting, fatigue, fever, headaches, chills, joint pain, and itchy skin. 3. Egyptian parents tried to protect their children with breastfeeding, spells, potions, and amulets.

CHAPTER 18

Cast of Characters

Ramesses II: Egyptian king who fought the Hittites; known as "The Great"

Nefertari: Ramesses's favorite wife

Menna: Ramesses's shield bearer

What Happened When?

Year 5: Ramesses led his army against the Hittites at Qadesh. Year 21: Egypt and Hatti negotiated a peace treaty. Ramesses ruled during the 19th Dynasty. The 19th Dynasty began in the 13th century BCE.

Word Bank   division; fraternity; treaty; regnal

Students' sentences should use *allegiance* and *rendezvous*.

Critical Thinking

The Egyptian army stopped to rest in the Wood of Labwi and set up camp. SO The Egyptians found two Hittite deserters hiding in the Wood of Labwi. The Hittite deserters told Ramesses that the Hittite king was too frightened of Ramesses to proceed further. SO Ramesses believed the deserters and took one division of the army toward Qadesh. The Army of Re did not know that they were vulnerable and in mortal danger. SO The Army of Re marched into a trap. The Egyptian patrol captured two Hittite spies who told them that the Hittite king and army were just over the hill. SO Ramesses knew that he had been tricked.Hittite charioteers charged the Army of Re. SO The Army of Re soldiers panicked and scattered. The Army of Re fled the battlefield. SO The Army of Re led the Hittite army directly toward Ramesses II and the Army of Amen.

Working with Primary Sources

1. Probably not all of what was written in the inscription was true, but some of it might have been true. 2. The royal scribes probably wrote this story to glorify their king and Egypt.

All Over the Map   1.–2. Check students' work against map on page 129. 3. Qadesh was strategically placed between the kingdoms of Hatti, Mesopotamia, and Egypt. Whoever controlled Qadesh could control the trade and make money from it.

CHAPTER 19

Word Bank   incense; necropolis; tell   Students' sentences should include *floodplain*.

Critical Thinking

Features of an Egyptian house: mud bricks, fleas, brick oven, bed, candles, sack of beans, red door, cloth door, people sleeping on roof, entrance hall, onions. Ask students to show their blueprints of Egyptian houses.

Comprehension

1. Egyptians burned incense to cover the smells of garbage and excrement from the street. 2. The houses at Deir el-Medina were nicer because the residents were well-paid tomb builders and their families. 3. Barter is exchanging goods of equal value, rather than paying for goods with money. 4. The back of the house, where the oven was, was extremely hot.

Do the Math   1. 32 gallons a day 2. 320 gallons a week

Working with Primary Sources

Students' biographical sketches will vary but should be supported by the details in the ostraca.

CHAPTER 20

Cast of Characters

Ramesses III: king of Egypt who successfully defended the country against the Sea Peoples

What Happened When?

The Sea Peoples had lost their homelands for unknown reasons, and were at that time rampaging through the region destroying towns and kingdoms.

Word Bank   javelin; maneuver; mortuary   *Mortal* can mean "causing death" or "not living forever." Students' sentences will vary.

Critical Thinking

Sea Peoples: disorderly and chaotic, conquered the Hittites, boats with sails, homeless. *Egyptians:* used archers, used grappling hooks, boats with oars, orderly rows, could lose their homeland. *Both:* charioteers, swords and spears.

Comprehension

Students' outlines will vary but should include main ideas and details from the chapter.

Write About It

The Egyptian advantages included boats that were powered by oars which made them more maneuverable in the Nile river mouths. They also seemed to have a better strategy of driving the Sea Peoples' boats toward their archers on shore. The Egyptians' style of using grappling hooks to capsize their opponent's boats also was an advantage.

CHAPTER 21

Cast of Characters

Strabo: Greek geographer who wrote *Geographia*, a description of the world as it was then known. The story of Rhodopis is like the story of Cinderella.

What Happened When?

King Tut's silver trumpet was restored and played on BBC Radio in 1939.

Word Bank   sacred ratio; innovator   Students's sentences should include *percussion*.

Critical Thinking

Nature: nautilus shell spiral, galaxies, sunflowers, pinecones, human body. *Egyptian Art:* jewelry, tombs, hieroglyphs, temples, pyramids. Students should understand that Egyptians would consider the ratio "sacred" because it is found throughout nature, and their gods, who were sacred, were also found throughout nature.

Working with Primary Sources

Rhodopis was kidnapped and sold to a kind old Egyptian. The other servants were mean to Rhodopis. The old man bought beautiful shoes for Rhodopis. Rhodopis had too many chores to go to the king's party. Horus, disguised as a falcon, snatched one of the shoes from Rhodopis and flew away. Horus dropped the shoe in the king's lap. The king searched for the woman who could wear the beautiful shoe. The shoe fit Rhodopis, and she pulled the other one from her tunic.

Comprehension

1. We know that Egyptians loved music because tombs and temple walls are covered with images of dancers and musicians. 2. Egyptian instruments included drums, cymbals, tambourines, flutes, trumpets, harps, lyres, and lutes. Students' paragraphs will vary.

CHAPTER 22

Cast of Characters

Strabo: Greek geographer who named the area in southern Egypt and northern Sudan "Nubia," after the Nuba people who roamed there

Piye (also known as Piankhi): king of Kush who united Egypt under his rule in the middle of the 8th century BCE

What Happened When?

about 747–716 BCE: rule of King Piye

about 20 CE: when Strabo gave Kush the name "Nubia"

Word Bank ambassador; contempt; obligation   Students' sentences should use *nomadic*.

Critical Thinking

Kush's archers were very skilled, SO the Egyptians called it *Ta-Seti*, "The Land of the Bow." Kush had gold mines, SO it became a wealthy and strong country. Egypt became very fractured and disorganized, SO it lost respect in the ancient world. The priests at Thebes became very powerful, SO the pharaoh's power was weakened. King Piye appointed his sister "the Divine Wife of the God," SO she became ruler of Upper Egypt.

Comprehension

1. The Greek word for *Nubia* is *Ethiopia*, which means "Land of the Burnt Faces." 2. During the Third Intermediate Period, the priesthood was passed down from father to son. 3. The Libyans, Nubians, Persians, Greeks, and Romans conquered Egypt. 4. *Sema-tawy* means "Uniter of Two Lands." Students' adjectives for King Piye and explanations will vary.

All Over the Map 1. Compare students' work with map on page 151. 2. Students should show that Wenamun traveled up the Nile to the Mediterranean, and then along the coast to Dor. 3. He probably traveled about 500 miles.

CHAPTER 23

Cast of Characters

Alexander the Great: King of Macedon who conquered Egypt and parts of Asia

Aristotle: teacher of Alexander

Plutarch: Greek biographer who wrote about the life of Alexander

Arrian: Roman historian born in Greece who wrote about Alexander

The titles of the two poems by Homer are the *Iliad* and the *Odyssey*.

What Happened When?

336 BCE: Alexander became king of Macedon when his father was assassinated.

late October 332 BCE: Alexander entered Egypt.

November 14, 332 BCE: Alexander was anointed pharaoh of Egypt.

April 331 BCE: Alexander left Egypt.

Word Bank odyssey; tribute; invincible   Students' sentences should include *descendant* and *oasis*.

Critical Thinking

Students' outlines will vary but should include main ideas and details from the chapter.

Working with Primary Sources

Possible answers: The king means that Alexander is meant for bigger things than the small kingdom of Macedon. The king feels that Alexander will become a great conqueror. Have students share with the class the information they discovered about "Achilles' heel."

CHAPTER 24

Cast of Characters

General Ptolemy: Alexander's general who ruled Egypt

Ptolemy III: king of Egypt who wanted to collect all the books in the world

Eratosthenes: mathematician who was librarian at Alexandria

Pliny the Elder: Roman historian who wrote about Pharos

Sostrates: architect of the lighthouse at Pharos

Ptolemy II: Greek king of Egypt

Ptolemy XII: Greek king of Egypt; father of Cleopatra

Berenice: daughter of Ptolemy XII, who had her killed

Cleopatra VII: daughter of Ptolemy XII who promoted learning in Alexandria

Julius Caesar: ruler of Rome who fell in love with Cleopatra

Mark Antony: ruler of Rome who fell in love with Cleopatra

Archimedes: mathematician and inventor who worked in Alexandria

Euclid: mathematician who worked in Alexandria

Heron: mathematician who worked in Alexandria

Ptolemy: geographer who worked in Alexandria

Aristarcus of Samos: astronomer who worked in Alexandria

What Happened When?

Ask students to show work. Students should have the periods in Egypt's history listed in correct order, and should write comments about each period.

Do the Math 3020 years

Word Bank stellar; parchment; opulence; ambition   The verb *muse* means "to think." Students' sentences will vary.

Critical Thinking Students' outlines will vary, but should include main ideas and details from the chapter.

Printed in the USA
CPSIA information can be obtained
at www.ICGtesting.com
LVHW082330040824
787359LV00010B/966